Modern Library Chronicles

LONDON

A. N. WILSON

LONDON

A History

A MODERN LIBRARY CHRONICLES BOOK

THE MODERN LIBRARY

NEW YORK

2004 Modern Library Edition

Copyright © 2004 by A. N. Wilson

All rights reserved under International and Pan-American
Copyright Conventions. Published in the United States by
Modern Library, an imprint of The Random House Publishing
Group, a division of Random House, Inc., New York,
and simultaneously in Canada by Random House
of Canada Limited, Toronto.

MODERN LIBRARY and the TORCHBEARER Design are registered
trademarks of Random House, Inc.

Originally published in Great Britain by Weidenfeld &
Nicolson, London.

Grateful acknowledgment is made to *The Independent* for
permission to reprint excerpts from an article by Jemima Lewis,
first published in *The Independent* January 22, 2004, copyright
© 2004 by *The Independent*, and excerpts from an article
by Johann Hari, first published in *The Independent*
January 22, 2004, copyright © 2004 by *The Independent*. Reprinted
by permission of *The Independent*.

3139 4926 1/05

LIBRARY OF CONGRESS CATALOGING-IN-PUBLICATION DATA

Wilson, A. N.
London: a history / A. N. Wilson.
p. cm.
Includes bibliographical references and index.
ISBN 0-679-64266-8
1. London (England)—History.   I. Title.

DA677.W55 2004   942.1—dc22   2004044836

Modern Library website address:
www.modernlibrary.com

Printed in the United States of America on acid-free paper

2   4   6   8   9   7   5   3   1

To Peter Ackroyd

CONTENTS

PRELUDE:
A
LONDON HISTORY

One of the best ways to see London, at once and as a whole, is to climb Hampstead Heath and look down from Parliament Hill. On a clear day, from this northern vantage point, the eye can stretch across the teeming, chaotic expanse, taking in familiar landmarks, such as the winking giant tower of Canary Wharf to the east, or the dome of St. Paul's directly ahead, or, to the west, the Palace of Westminster and the Abbey. From this height, we see the northern conurbations of Kentish Town and Camden Town immediately beneath us, we see Regent's Park dotted with trees, and Hyde Park and, far beyond, south of the river, we can look to the suburban sprawl of south London, its terraced houses, its villas, its tower blocks, its churches and cinemas.

What we are looking at is not a city which has been built according to one uniform plan. Here is no grid of numbered streets as in New York, no architectural homogeneity as in St. Petersburg, no rigidly pure urban plan as in post-Napoleonic, post-Haussmann Paris. We see, rather, a group of boroughs, former villages, bursting with life and vigor, but existing in barely controlled social and architectural chaos. From where we stand, with the natural beauties of the Heath behind us, we see little of beauty. This is not one of the great city views of the world, such as we might take in from the Pincio or Fiesole when gazing upon Rome or Florence. Little that we look upon would seem to have been planned. The two great centers of old London—the City of London itself, the square mile, in the east; and the city of Westminster, to the west—are distinct, even today. The villages, swollen to boroughs, which surround and join them by a multitude of overcrowded, trafficky streets, all have their own identity and history.

The history of London is therefore by its very nature a collective history, a kaleidoscope of many stories rather than a book with one author or one theme. Moreover, because of the size and fluidity of London's population, because of its constant change and growth, much of its story is hidden from us. Workmen gouging out the earth for a new building can suddenly unearth for us evidence of a lost London, the outlines of an old theater where Shakespeare acted, the conduit of a medieval waterway, or paving of Roman times. Sentiment will always be stirred by such discoveries and, in some cases, the few fragments of a forgotten past will be preserved or reclaimed by archaeology. One suspects that there have been many more cases in the history of London's construction industry when, to avoid delays on the new building, the pick or the electric drill has merely obliterated the vestiges of the old in order to make way for the new.

Most London history, like the lives of most Londoners, has passed into oblivion, and what we choose to recover of it, especially in so short a study as this, will be arbitrary. Even as we stand here on Parliament Hill, looking down on the London of the twenty-first century, we become aware of how much is concealed, how much has gone forever. We can see the physical properties of London geography, for example. From this height we can see that the cluster of conurbations which we call London grows up on and around a group of low hills: but although we catch a glimpse of silver sunlight on the great Thames, which snakes between the gray buildings, we see nothing of the rivers and streams that once flowed down from its hills: the Wandle and the Effra, still visible in south London; the Walbrook running through Shoreditch, through the

City and down to the Thames; the Tyburn, rising in Belsize Park and flowing—no more—down Haverstock Hill, through Regent's Park and on, beneath Buckingham Palace. These streams, like the stories of millions of dead Londoners, are now lost to us, hidden from view, dried up or, like the Fleet river, gone underground.

The Fleet, another tributary of the Thames, had its origin in the Hampstead ponds of Caen Wood, or Kenwood, just behind where we stand on Parliament Hill looking down on present-day London. Were we to follow the course of the Fleet, almost every phase of London history would unfold before us.

———

The western head of the Fleet rose in the Vale of Health (said to derive its name from being unaffected by the Great Plague of 1665), the eastern in the park of what is now Kenwood House. These parts of London, grassy and wooded, remind us of how, until Victorian times, there was an edge, an ending to London's urban sprawl, which was truly rural. When Mr. Pickwick and his friends speculated on the source of the Hampstead Ponds, they were talking not of a rich suburb but of a country village.

Even as late as the 1840s the Fleet, in passing Kentish Town and Gospel Oak, was a stream in open country. The Gospel Oak was so named because preachers once spoke beneath its boughs. Tradition has it that St. Augustine himself, bringing the faith from Rome in the very late sixth century, was the first such evangelist. We do not know whether that is true, or whether he laid the altar stone of what is one of the oldest churches in England, old St. Pancras. (Some say this church, on the banks of the Fleet river, dates from as early as A.D. 313 or 314.) The Fleet, like the story of London itself, is by now subterranean: it crosses under the Regent's Canal and at points is buried as deep as twenty-five feet. By the time it flowed south of St. Pancras Church it had surfaced again. The district known as Battlebridge derived its name from a single-tracked brick structure crossing the Fleet.

Which battle the name commemorates, no one knows. The tradition that it marks the spot of Boadicea's last stand against the Romans is fanciful, as is the conjecture believed by some Londoners that that redoubtable warrior lies deep beneath the ground of what is now Platform Seven at King's Cross Station. In 1830, when George IV died, the inhabitants of Battlebridge erected an octagonal building decorated with pilasters to commemorate that not always popular king. It was completed by about 1836. Some called it, by virtue of the weather vane cross on its roof, Boadicea's Cross, others St. George's Cross, and others still, perhaps unaccountably attributing sanctity to the departed Hanoverian, King's Cross. A stucco statue said to resemble this monarch was seen above its doorway. No obvious purpose for the octagon was found. It was used as a police station, then as a pub, then as a camera obscura. With the coming of the railways, the building was found to be in the way and it was demolished in 1845. "King's Cross" had been in existence for less than ten years, but it has ever since given its name to one of London's seediest parts.

The Fleet crossed what is now King's Cross Road and flowed down towards the Farringdon Road. In this part of its journey, it was called the Hol-bourne or Healing Stream. It was also known as the River of Wells. In its journey from Hampstead to King's Cross, the Fleet has reminded us that London is a collection of villages and towns which until the Railway Age was adjacent to, and indeed part of, open country, farmland. It has reminded us of London's Roman origin and its very ancient Christian past. It has symbolized, by vanishing, the extent to which the railway age, with its concomitant industrialization and overpopulation, changed London forever, destroying and hiding much of its distinctive and lingering past. But as we follow the River of Wells towards the Thames, we meet other aspects of London history. At Lamb's Conduit, which linked the Holborn (Fleet) to a little stream, we are reminded of the wealth of the guilds in the Tudor Age—for it was William Lamb, of the Guild of Clothworkers (Gentleman of the Chapel to Henry VIII), who built this little waterway, once thick with watercress, to irrigate the neighborhood. At nearby Clerkenwell, we remember an earlier London which the Tudor merchants opposed and changed— for by this *fons Clericorum* (well of clerics) medieval miracle plays were performed, and the Benedictine nuns, as well as the Prior and Brethren of the Order of St. John of Jerusalem, esteemed and used the cleansing properties of the wells.

In later times, the polluted Fleet river was a byword for filth and corruption, a potent symbol for the moral stench of the capital city. Ben Jonson, in the days when the Fleet was still navigable, wondered in 1616,

> … How dare your daintie nostrils (in so hot a season
> When every clerke eates artichokes and peason,
> Laxative lettus, and such windie meate)
> Tempt such a passage?

Pope in the *Dunciad* could see the changes which had come upon the River of Wells since St. Bridget's or St. Brideswell had cleansed and nourished the medieval Dominican priory, or Blackfriars. In 1728, Pope wrote

> Fleet-ditch with disemboguing streams
> Rolls the large tribute of dead dogs to Thames,
> The King of Dykes! than whom, no sluice of mud,
> With deeper sable blots the silver flood.
> "Here strip, my children! Here at once leap in,
> Here prove who best can dash thro thick and thin."

The scatological humor, the ugly baptism of the Dunces in excrement, was a prophetic harbinger of the "gutter press," which would establish itself in Fleet Street two and three hundred years after Pope's comedy of the engrimed hack writers.

There exists in the Guildhall Library a pencil sketch of 1837 by Anthony Crosby, based on the recollections of two very old men in the Charterhouse, of the Fleet Bridge at Fleet Street, with boatmen punting in the fetid, viscous waters, and the old Fleet Market still visible. In the eighteenth century, the Fleet river was still used to transport "great quantities of corn" to the market. Yet the demands of street traffic, coach parks, storage space, and rubbish dumps inevitably led to the filling in of wharves and the building of low bridges, and whole streets, over the Fleet. The Fleet Market went in 1829. So too, in the 1840s, did the old Fleet Prison, in whose walls, as in the waters of the Fleet itself, the very history of London could be read.

Prison, until a late stage in British history, was used as a punishment only in a minority of criminal cases. The chief function of prisons was to hold accused persons or political dissidents in custody until they could be punished, corporally or capitally. This prison, which dates from the time of William the Conqueror, was used in medieval times for what we would call remand prisoners, those awaiting trial. (It was the chief of four prisons along the Fleet, the others being Ludgate Prison, Cold Bath Fields Prison, and Bridewell Prison.) The medieval prisoners seem, from the records in the Rolls, to have been for the most part minor offenders—for debt, disputes about land, and breaches of marital promise. No felons were incarcerated here before the Renaissance period, nor was any prisoner clapped in irons. The most famous medieval prisoner is fictitious: Sir John Falstaff. "Go, carry Sir John Falstaffe to the Fleete," commands the Lord Chief Justice at the end of *Henry IV, Part Two.*

In the reign of Queen Mary, in September 1553, we find imprisoned there Miles Coverdale, the man whose translations of the Psalms are still sung daily in the cathedrals and colleges of England. "This day appeared before the Lordes, John Hooper, Bishop of Gloucester, and Miles Coverdale, Bishop of Exon." After Catholic Mary persecuted Protestant heroes, her sister, Elizabeth, in the next reign, here incarcerated Catholics. We read in 1582 that the Recorder of London prosecuted one Osborn, a priest and Franciscan friar, for saying mass in the Fleet, where many of his fellow Catholics were imprisoned. It was in the reign of Elizabeth that torture was first used in England. If in the 1580s those maltreated were Catholics, by 1620–21 we read of the Warden of the Fleet, Alexander Harris, persecuting Puritans. Prisoners were now caged and locked in irons.

The old Fleet Prison was destroyed in the Great Fire of 1666. The rebuilt prison witnessed the great century—the eighteenth—of crime and punishment in England. By modern standards there was an extraordinary blend of liberty and brutality in an eighteenth-century prison, reflected in the gallows humor of novels and poems. Upon arrival, a prisoner would be forced to pay his keep, and if money was not forthcoming he would be stripped of his coat; this was called putting down your Garnish. The place was filthy, and if you fell foul of the warden you could find yourself in irons, tortured, whipped, or confined in dung heaps. Beside and against this disagreeable state of affairs was the fact that there were a chapel and a billiards room; in the yard you could play skittles, mississippi (a game like bagatelle), fives, or tennis. On Monday night there was a wine club and on Thursday night a beer club. In 1774, when there were 213 prisoners, the overcrowding in the place was caused by the fact that the incarcerated were joined by their wives and children.

Dickens in *Barnaby Rudge* vividly recalls for us the dramatic moment when the "No Popery" riots of 1780, orchestrated by Lord George Gordon, turned their attentions to the Newgate and Fleet prisons. The Fleet Prison was burnt to the ground, but rebuilt in 1781–82, and in Victorian times it was one of the many debtors' prisons. It was a humiliation to be put in one of these places (witness Dickens's shame at his father's time in the Marshalsea Prison, richly tapped in *Little Dorrit*), but in some ways it must have been restful to abandon the capitalist treadmill and become a debtor in the Fleet in the early decades of the nineteenth century. There was a begging grate at the bottom of Ludgate Hill where a prisoner stood collecting money from passersby. It was adorned with the legend "Pray Remember poor Debtors. No Allowance."

In the Middle Ages, the crimes which brought men to the Fleet were comparatively minor misunderstandings over contracts; in the Tudor Age, men and women here fell victim to the religious bigotry of the times and were persecuted for being Catholic, or Protestant; in the great age of commerce the Fleet Prison locked you up for debt. In an age guided by Adam Smith, the worst heresy you could commit was not against God but against Mammon.

So the Fleet Prison was done away; and the life of the Fleet river in Victorian times reflected the preoccupations of a resourceful age—the Victorian desire to improve, expand, reform, cleanse. It was the fate of the Fleet river to be incorporated into those most ingenious feats of Victorian engineering: the London sewers. Once Dr. John Snow had established beyond question, in 1854, that the plague of cholera was waterborne, the case for urgent action was established. The authorities took their time. The Metropolitan Board of Works was established in 1855, with Joseph Bazalgette as chief engineer; he devised a system of interconnecting sewers which covered the entire capital.

Even so, this system was not built until, after 1858, the

"Great Stink" of the Thames was so intolerable that while the Houses of Parliament in Westminster were in session the windows overlooking the river had to be draped with curtains soaked in chloride of lime to allow members to breathe. Bazalgette's sewerage network was entirely new, but it incorporated and finally concealed the waters of the Fleet, which had been gazed upon by Roman legionaries and by the first Christian missionaries; by crusaders and medieval nuns; by Tudor merchants and the City traders of the eighteenth century.

The Fleet did not go quietly. In 1846, when it was still an open sewer carrying its reeking load from north London to the Thames, it burst its drain and overflowed into the cellars on the west side of Farringdon Street. In the lower parts of Clerkenwell, household furniture, cattle, and three poorhouses were caught in the eddying stench and swept away in a torrent of ordure. When the railways penetrated Clerkenwell, the river took its revenge. The construction of the London Underground disturbed the old waters. (The Tyburn is piped across the line at Baker Street, as is the Westbourne at Sloane Square Station.) In 1862, the Fleet undermined the embankment at Clerkenwell and burst into the railway, "filling the tunnel with sewage for a great distance."

Yet many office workers who board or leave their train at Farringdon Station today will be unaware of the Fleet's existence and of its continued life, still making damp the basements of the buildings along the Farringdon Road.

———

London history, like its lost rivers, is hidden beneath the surface of its present streets, railways, offices, shops, flats, and houses. It is the way of histories of London to emphasize the continuity between past and present. The sensation of London's spirits continuing to haunt the very stones of the place underlies Peter Ackroyd's brilliant evocations of the London past in such novels as *Hawksmoor* and *Dr. Dee*.

Yet though it would be a very insensitive person who was not aware, in journeying about the capital, of London's rich antiquity, it is possible, surely, to believe that we have, in quite recent times, entered a phase which is completely new. The history is there, hidden like the lost rivers, but in all effective senses it has been obliterated by what London in the last half century has done to itself.

Until fifty years ago, London's wealth derived from two principal sources—the manufacturing industry, and the great financial institutions of the City: the City of London proper, the stock exchange, the private banks and insurance companies and City traders. The truly stupendous wealth once generated by manufacturing in London has, today, all but died out, with no hope of revival. The City, capital C, has, during the same period, changed totally. After the "Big Bang" in 1986 and the deregulation of the stock exchange, the geographical location of the trading floors and brokers' offices remained a matter of convenience, not necessity. The advent of the computer made it largely unnecessary to have a physical stock exchange at all. As for the great banks and insurance companies that were once all or nearly all owned by British families, they have been sold to or absorbed by giant companies from Germany and America. The City of London, once a bastion of British fiscal and economic independence, is now effectively owned by foreign money. For all the pageantry of the City— the Annual Procession of the Lord Mayor in his golden coach, the arcane ceremonies at Guildhall and the City companies— the City survives entirely because its survival happens to suit its non-British controllers.

The chief "industry" of the rest of London is tourism. Millions, with cameras draped around their necks, troop through the Tower, St. Paul's Cathedral, and Westminster Abbey each year, spending billions of pounds in all the hotels and restaurants that have sprung up to accommodate their requirements. It is a matter of judgment whether these tourists come to see London's past, or visit London for other reasons. In any event, now that London has become a tourist center, this very fact has destroyed much of its historic character. The Tower, for example, is no longer really a fortress. Its function *is* that of a tourist attraction. The tourists make its real history and function seem as ersatz as Disney World.

While these huge changes in the economic climate and composition of London were being effected, two other great changes were also happening. The first, begun by Hitler's Luftwaffe and gleefully continued by two generations of modernist architects, was the destruction and rebuilding of old London. For the most part, the new buildings that have sprung up, when compared with the magnificence of Manhattan or Chicago, are staggeringly undistinguished. There is hardly a corner of the British capital where such nondescript but at the same time intrusive building has not gone on. The Square Mile of the City has all but been obliterated by it. Look down upon London, as we did at the beginning of this chapter, from Hampstead Heath, and a great splurge of needlessly dreary buildings spreads itself at your feet: hospitals, schools, roads, blocks of flats, everywhere from the Isle of Dogs to Chiswick, from Hampstead to Sydenham—badly executed, badly designed, and ugly, ugly, ugly.

Those who inhabit this place are, some of them, holders of British passports, but increasingly not. In the last ten years London has witnessed the phenomenon of asylum seekers on a scale unrivaled by any other city in the world. Hundreds of thousands of Londoners are now visitors who have arrived, without sanction, from Eastern Europe and elsewhere. Their arrival has been coincident with a colossal increase in crime, and a near crippling of such resources as council-owned housing, hospitals, and schools. There has also been, in the last half century, a huge legal immigration to London by

British passport holders from the West Indies, from Pakistan, India, Bangladesh, Africa, and the Far East.

Philosophers like to debate whether the ax that has had three new handles and seven new heads is the same ax. Some who survey the history of London will decide that, mysteriously, the spirit of London—William Blake's or Peter Ackroyd's London, as it were—goes on, whatever huge changes we have described in the economy, the architectural structure, and the demography. Others might think that the London of old has actually died—or at best, gone underground—to be replaced by a confused, overcrowded multinational conurbation which shares the same name but has nothing whatever in common with the London of Nicholas Hawksmoor, Charles Dickens, or Marie Lloyd.

2

NEW TROY
OR
ROMAN LONDON?

One of the favorites of King Richard II impeached by the Merciless Parliament of 1388 was a former Lord Mayor of London, Sir Nicholas Brembre (or Bramber). The King's uncle, Gloucester, was determined to prove that Brembre, an old enemy, had done something worthy of death, accusing him of tyrannous conduct during his mayoralty and of threatening behavior during elections. He had, Gloucester alleged, filled the Guildhall with armed men to prevent his opponents on the Corporation coming to vote, uttering the warlike cry of "Tuwez, tuwez!" None of these charges could be made to stick. Brembre had made enemies while Lord Mayor, for example the aldermen he turned out of the Common Council, but he had also made friends among those he appointed to offices (such as his comptroller in the Port of London, Geoffrey Chaucer) and the King, who, under Brembre's mayoralty, had been lent a much needed four thousand marks.[1]

Brembre, a grocer who had been hugely enriched by his friendship with the King, acquiring estates in Mereworth, Maplescomb, and West Peckham in Kent, was proud of his knighthood and elected to be tried, at his impeachment, by battle. The lords refused, but when they all crammed into Westminster Hall for his trial, on February 17, 1388, they insisted on giving him a fair hearing. The King himself made a speech in his favor, which infuriated the appellants. (Eleven years later, in this very hall, Richard II would depose himself with a moving speech; Shakespeare immortalizes the moment.) On this occasion, his intervention did his favorite no good. Brembre was sent back to imprisonment in the Tower of London, whence the marshal should take him from the said City of London—"lui treyner parmye la dite cité de Loundres, et avant tan q'as ditz Fourches [Tyburn], et illeoqs lui prendre par le cool" (lawyers, the King, and his courtiers all conducted their business, in the late fourteenth century, in French).[2]

Brembre was only one of many Londoners before and since who made his last journey down the course of what is now Oxford Street to Tyburn to be hanged by the neck. Today, as we go on the top of a bus from Selfridges to Marble Arch, we might sometimes reflect on those who trundled in the same direction in a cart, to the jeering or cheering of crowds, to meet this grisly fate. Brembre, like almost all of them, is a forgotten figure today.

One detail from his trial arrests our attention. As Gloucester's witnesses brought more and more outlandish complaints against the knightly grocer, one of them claimed that he had referred to London as "the New Troy." It remains obscure, at this date, why this had seemed so damaging. Perhaps the witness remembered that the old Troy had gone up in flames, so that the appellation seemed seditious.

Certainly Brembre did not invent the idea of London as the New Troy. Geoffrey of Monmouth, in his *History of the Kings of Britain,* tells how one Brutus, a Trojan warrior, is told by the goddess Diana that "beyond the setting of the sun, past the realms of Gaul, there lies an island in the sea, once occupied by giants. Now it is empty and ready for your folk. Down the years this will prove an abode suited to you and to your people; and for your descendants it will be a second Troy. A race of kings will be born there from your stock and the round circle of the whole earth will be subject to them."[3] Geoffrey of Monmouth (d. 1155) was a Celt and he gloried in the idea that

London owed its origin to a legendary hero named Brutus or Brut, the eponymous founder of Brut—or Britain.

Modern chroniclers, guided by the archaeologists and by the Roman historian Cassius Dio, have attributed the origins of London to the Romans. Julius Caesar passed through, during his invasion of 54 B.C., and might well have seen Gauls in mud-and-wattle huts settling on the banks of the Thames, but it is the invasion of A.D. 43 that signaled the arrival of Romans as a permanency. London was occupied, or founded, by Aulus Plautius, the first governor of Britain, who seems to have enabled his emperor, Claudius, to cross the river at a site undetermined. (The first Roman bridge over the river was in the Southwark/City area, but most scholars seem to believe that Claudius crossed farther upstream, near Westminster.)

There remain abundant traces of Roman London. The City Wall, built of Kentish ragstone, may still be seen at Tower Hill, in St. Alphage's churchyard, and at London Wall. Nothing survives of the large basilica and forum, built over a site of eight acres and the largest north of the Alps. But in 1954, on the now dry banks of the Walbrook, one of London's lost rivers, were found the remains of a Temple of Mithras, with many artefacts—heads of Mithras the bull slayer, Serapis, and Minerva; a group of Bacchus and his companions; a silver canister; an incense strainer; a relief of Mithras killing the bull. At the north end of Lower Thames Street, a Roman bath was discovered, and there are mosaic pavements under a number of City buildings, including 11 Ironmonger Lane and the Bank of England.

The formidable British warrior queen Boudicca, or Boadicea, could massacre legionaries and make her furious last stand in a battle in London in A.D. 60, but she was warring against the inevitable. In Roman times, Britain was wholly a "part of Europe," as the modern phrase has it. A tombstone in the Guildhall Museum shows a relief of a gentleman wearing a toga. Tacitus tells us these marks of Romanness were worn everywhere in Romano-British cities. Life was clearly civilized, to judge from the beautiful Roman samian vase, late second century, discovered in Southwark, or the Roman beaker decorated with a leaping stag, unearthed in Jewry Street.

In its glory days, Roman London probably numbered 25,000 inhabitants and was perhaps the fifth largest city of the northern provinces. It was essentially the product of Romans' needs and skills. They needed to bring their ships as far up the estuary as possible, and to unload men and goods at a point where they could be dispersed to the rest of the country. For two miles along the northern foreshore, from what is now the Tower of London to Waterloo Bridge, was a firm gravel terrace ideal for their purpose. But the point of London was lost on more primitive peoples who could not build fortifications or roads to match those of the Romans. The saucer-shaped London basin, stretching from the Chilterns to the North Downs, was, for the primitive tribesmen of Britain, not merely vulnerable to attack but thickly wooded and clayey (hence difficult to cultivate).

When the last legions vanished in 410, London began to crumble. When in 601 St. Augustine arrived with a different form of Roman conquest to baptize the Germanic settlers, he would have found the Roman city in ruins. The Saxons never made bricks; their houses, and most of their churches, would have been of wattle and daub. Though some revival took place during the times of Alfred the Great, and the Danish king Cnut, it was not really until the Norman Conquest that London could be said to resume a history worthy of the name.

3

NORMAN LONDON

The tourist to London wants to see the Tower of London and Westminster Abbey. Both were creations of the Normans, though the present Abbey Church dates from the reign of Henry III and was begun in 1245. Before William the Conqueror entered London, Edward the Confessor (1042–1066) had founded the Benedictine monastery on the Isle of Thorns (Thorney). Edward was English on his father's side, Norman-French on his mother's, and from a cultural point of view the Conquest began in his reign and with his founding of this abbey. The monks, many of them, were French. Their handwriting was French. Their seals were French. When William conquered England in the year of Edward's death, he carried on the great building work of his cousin the saintly Confessor, and the abbey church contains Edward's shrine.

There was enormous significance in the fact that Duke William of Normandy, the Conqueror, chose to be crowned King of England in Westminster. This great monastic church has witnessed the coronation of all the kings and queens of England save two Edwards (the Fifth, who was murdered in the Tower as a child, and the Eighth, who abdicated).

The Coronation Chair dates from the time of Edward I. Having conquered Scotland, he had designed a chair which was to be placed in God's House in Westminster and which would contain the holy stone. This stone was a relic of great importance to the vanquished Scots; some said it was the very pillow on which St. Columba had rested his head. It was

brought south with the greatest solemnity. Scottish national-
ists have resented its seizure ever since, because it came as a
symbol of the fact, expressed by the metrical legend of Sir
William Wallace, "Quhar that Stayne is, Scotti's suld master
be." But throne and stone were designed to be all of a piece.
The ancient stone upon which the kings of Scotland had been
proclaimed, time out of mind, should now be contained, as in
a reliquary (which is what the holy chair is) beside the shrine
of St. Edward the Confessor. It was placed in an elevated position and looked down the Abbey like a bishop's throne,
speaking of the link, from the very beginning, between the
peoples of the British Isles, united under God and under the
Crown of Westminster.

When they were opening the devolved Scottish Assembly
in 1999, Prime Minister John Major, a latter-day iconoclast to
rival the Puritan vandals who attacked the Abbey in the reign
of Charles I, tore out the stone and without ceremony sent it
back to Scotland, not to be placed in a position of sacred
honor but just as an exhibit. The symbolism of seven hundred
years was mindlessly destroyed in an afternoon.

Westminster Abbey, magnificent as it remains, both as one
of the finest Gothic churches in Christendom and as our national Valhalla, with its many tombs of heroes, statesmen,
poets, musicians, had lost something irreplaceable. It had
ceased to be a shrine and become a tourist attraction.

———

The Bayeux Tapestry, that strip cartoon woven to depict the
Norman Conquest, shows a comet in the sky hovering over
the Abbey, seeing the Abbey as the symbol of the new era that
was coming to London and to England. Over the Confessor's
Abbey, a man grasps its weathercock with one hand, while the
other rests on the roof of the Palace of Westminster.

From the start of the Norman administration the seat of

government was at Westminster, which in those days was more or less an island, connected to the mainland by a narrow isthmus at the point where, now, Birdcage Walk enters Great George Street.

The Palace of Westminster is so called because it was here that the kings lived. It was here that they summoned their parliaments of lords spiritual (bishops) and temporal. Westminster Hall was completely redesigned in the reign of Richard II, but that great medieval building which we see today, and which has witnessed the lying in state of Sir Winston Churchill and of kings and queens, as well as many historic events such as the trial of Charles I, is built on the site of its predecessor. The first Westminster Hall, of 1097–99, was a rugged structure built in Caen stone. The distinctive white of this Norman stone was to become characteristic of London's great public buildings, though nearly all the great buildings from the seventeenth to the twentieth centuries were in Portland stone.

The white stone of Caen, however, was used to build the other famous London landmark that any tourist wants to see: namely, the Tower. If Westminster, the Norman capital, tells us that London was henceforward the seat of government, the Tower reminds us of the city's strategic importance. Since the Romans left, there had been no one with the skill to construct a truly effective port in the river basin, or to guard it from the strategic position of what is now Tower Hill. But this is what the Normans did, with one of the most magnificent of their castles.

The Tower was a fortress; its donjon or keep was the White Tower, whose Caen stone walls are fifteen feet thick. Its great complex of buildings, and its moat and its river frontage, are themselves the most eloquent possible history of London. This place, as well as being a fortress defending the port, has also been a royal palace, a treasury (it still guards the Crown Jewels), and, in early days, the Royal Mint.

If we are exploring early medieval London and trying to find out its essence and its history, we must briefly mention two other extraordinary survivals (or, in one case, half survival).

In Smithfield, near the great meat market and the Cloth Fair, is the abbey church of St. Bartholomew, a glorious piece of sturdy Romanesque whose nave rivals Durham or Peterborough Cathedral's. Next to this church is St. Bartholomew's Hospital, founded by the same monk, the Augustinian canon Rahere, who built the abbey. From 1123, this hospital was a place of healing for the sick. The same supposedly Conservative Government that ripped the Stone of Destiny from its reliquary in Westminster Abbey also proposed the closure of St. Bartholomew's Hospital, but luckily this death sentence was repealed.

The other great medieval building to consider here is the Temple Church. The Knights Templar wore white tunics adorned with red crosses, which showed them to be immune from all jurisdiction save that of the Pope. Their task was to protect pilgrims to the Holy Land. Their first London church was built in 1162; this one dates from 1185. The Round Church was constructed in imitation of the Holy Sepulcher in Jerusalem. It was damaged by German bombs in the Second World War, but luckily much of it has survived. It is a place with an extraordinarily powerful atmosphere, speaking of England's half-forgotten past.

The Temple, as the whole area was designated, passed out of the Templars' hands, and in the fourteenth century the Knights Hospitaller leased it to lawyers. Ever since, the Inns of Court have been found here, the Middle Temple and the Inner Temple. Not far away are the other surviving Inns of Court, Gray's Inn and Lincoln's Inn. The Inns are not pubs, as their name suggested, but colleges of lawyers, places where the law is studied and where the barristers congregate in their chambers to practice and dispute the law.

Thus we see that from the very earliest medieval times, London has been the center of government at Westminster. It has been a great trading port, protected by the Tower. It has been a great center of medicine and of the other profession, the law.

4

CHAUCER'S LONDON

The nursery rhyme about London Bridge falling down is a strange piece of folk memory of an Old Norse poem dating from the reign of Cnut—"London Bridge is broken down/Gold is won and bright renown." London Bridge, once built of stone in 1176, was not in the habit of falling down as often as "My fair lady" was informed. In fact, its massive structure survived until demolished in the reign of William IV. They pulled it down because it was too narrow for the volume of traffic it bore, and too encrusted with low arches. The only bridge downstream from Kingston until the eighteenth century, it was a place of trade, concourse, and residence, a bit like an enormous Rialto. Houses were built along it. The heads of traitors and criminals (parboiled and then dipped in tar to preserve them) adorned it. In the middle of the bridge was a chapel dedicated to the memory of Thomas Becket.

It was to worship at the shrine of Becket in Canterbury that Chaucer's pilgrims assembled:

> In Southwerk at the Tabard as I lay
> Redy to wenden on my pilgrymage
> To Caunterbury with ful devout corage ...

The tabard is a short jacket open at the sides, worn by a knight over his armor and emblazoned with his arms. It is also worn by heralds, in their case emblazoned with the royal arms. A good name for an inn in a city where so much pageantry and ceremony took place.

Southwark came into its own after the building of London Bridge. Its magnificent thirteenth-century church of St. Mary Overie (becoming a procathedral only in 1897 and Southwark Cathedral in 1905) is the first Gothic church in London, and the finest. All the region was owned by the bishops of Winchester. The colloquialism "clink" for a jail or prison was first given to the Bishop of Winchester's private prison, not far from St. Mary Overie, and there survives a fragment of rose window from the banqueting hall of the bishop's palace.

Geoffrey Chaucer (who died, aged about sixty, in 1400) is one of those very great artists who existed at the very hub of public life, while remaining detached and in many ways quite mysterious. We know what he looked like: a portrait survives. His nervous young colleague Hoccleve has given us an unforgettable picture of Chaucer at work, not as a poet but in the office. We possess more life records of him than we do of Shakespeare. Yet he still keeps his own smiling counsel. In the *Canterbury Tales,* the innkeeper upbraids him for his diffidence, his looking at the ground when he speaks and his inferiority as a poet—"Thy drasty rymyng is nat worth a toord!"

This ironical and amusing man was page to Lionel, Duke of Clarence (the third son of Edward III). He was widely traveled in France and Italy. He was involved with both sides of London life—the Westminster court, and the City with its trade and merchants. As clerk of works from 1389 to 1391, Chaucer would have helped oversee the rebuilding of Westminster Hall, with its superb double hammer-beam roof by Richard II's architect, Henry Yevele. As comptroller of the customs from 1374 to 1385, he lived in rooms above the gate at Aldgate and would have been a witness to all the comings and goings of the port and to all the tensions and rivalries between the different factions in the City and between the City and the court. He would have seen one of the most dramatic popular uprisings London ever knew, the Peasants' Revolt in

1381, when a vagrant priest called John Ball preached to a huge crowd on Blackheath and asked the subversive question

> When Adam dalf, and Eve span,
> Wo was thanne a gentilman?

The Kentish peasants were met by the fourteen-year-old King on Blackheath, and the Essex mob swarmed near Chaucer's Aldgate windows. The London mobs joined forces with their Kentish leader, Wat Tyler, who demanded the abolition of the peerage, while Jack Straw, another of the rebel leaders, was leading an attack on the Treasurer's house at Highbury. The boy king was very brave; he held a debate with Tyler at Smithfield, offering to be his captain and to abolish the aristocracy, but of course it was a ruse and the rising was eventually crushed.

The question posed by the rebel priest, however—who was a gentleman?—was of deep resonance for Chaucer's generation. For this poet-courtier, pageboy, and friend of monarchs was not the son of an aristocrat (though his granddaughter Alice became one of the very richest and most powerful women in England, as the Duchess of Suffolk).

Chaucer's father was a vintner, John Chaucer, described as a "citizen of London."[1] The house was in Thames Street by Walbrook, at or near the foot of Dowgate Hill. The principal sources of London's wealth in the Middle Ages were trade in cloth, both wool and silk, and wine. The wool and silk were brought upriver from all parts of the country and exported as cloth.

The City livery companies, which survive today with their halls, had their origins, most of them, in the Middle Ages, and their names reflect the range of trades and crafts most commonly and profitably practised in the City. The Vintners' Company, for example, received a charter in 1364, granting it a monopoly of trade with Gascony. The Merchant Taylors go back to 1327, the Mercers to 1347, the Drapers to 1364. The Pewterers, the Plumbers, the Skinners and the Wax Chandlers, the Saddlers and the Dyers are all medieval.

Many craft guilds had established themselves as early as the twelfth or thirteenth century. Liverymen, members of these companies, could wear a distinctive uniform and were granted the freedom of the city. From among their number were chosen the aldermen, who in turn chose the Lord Mayor. The first mayor, Henry Fitzailwin, a wealthy merchant, was in office for twenty years, from 1192 to 1212. King John was forced to concede the independence of the City, granting it its charter in 1215. John's son, Henry III, tried to claw back the privileges the City had claimed for itself, and Edward I all but abolished them. For thirteen years, 1284–97, he ruled the City directly through his own appointees. But this was the last time that happened, and for a very simple reason. Whenever a king needed money, he had to come cap in hand to the City to borrow it or be given it. We noted at the very beginning of this book the extent of Richard II's debt to the grocer Lord Mayor Sir Nicholas Brembre.

By the fifteenth century, the mayors were styling themselves Lord Mayor and the Guildhall was a splendid building. Its great library was collected with the money left by London's most famous mayor, Richard Whittington. One of the most stabilizing features of English life is that whereas the merchant class of other countries aspired to become gentry and aristocracy, the English landed classes, frequently poor, liked nothing more than to form connections with trade and money making. Snobbery about being "in trade" was a Victorian absurdity and would not have been comprehensible to Chaucer or Whittington. Whittington came from a Gloucestershire gentry family who apprenticed him as a mercer in London. He became mayor four times and made a fortune, which, since he was unmarried, he left to the city that had been the cause of his prosperity.

It is not clear how this solid and slightly boring figure became the Dick Whittington of puppet plays, cheap books, and ultimately Christmas pantomimes. There are Russian, Scandinavian, and even Buddhist cognate stories. Dick Whittington, an orphan boy, comes to London to work as a scullion to Hugh Fitzwarren and is helped by the kindness of Fitzwarren's daughter Alice and by his clever cat. Worn out by ill treatment from his mistress, he steals away from Leadenhall Street, but when he reaches Holloway he hears the merry peal of the Bow Bells, which seem to say, "Turn again Whittington, Lord Mayor of London."

The legend seems to have taken written form for the first time in the reign of James I. In 1605 a license was granted for the publication of a ballad called "The vertuous lyfe and memorable death of Sir Richard Whittington, mercer, sometyme Lord Mayor." There is a reference to it in Beaumont and Fletcher's play *The Knight of the Burning Pestle* (printed 1613). The story is in a sense a perennial London legend. Among all the lures the city has offered outsiders over the years—anonymity, sexual gratification, excitement, escape from the humdrum, or simply the opportunity to work—the most potent is the sense that the place can somehow work magic, making poor girls and boys rich, and transforming those who arrive in obscurity into figures who are wealthy and famous. The Lord Mayors of London continue today to be as solid, sensible, rich, and dependable as the real Richard Whittington. It is the legendary Dick who inspired the writers, pop stars, TV personalities, city slickers, and sharp politicians who over the generations have seen London as their means of asserting the will, of *getting on.*

5

TUDOR
AND
STUART LONDON

The Globe Theatre is a faithful reconstruction of the open-air playhouse designed in 1599, where Shakespeare worked and for which he wrote many of his greatest plays," says the website for Sam Wanamaker's building on the south side of the River Thames. "Today, audiences of 'this wooden O' sit in a gallery or stand informally as a groundling in the yard, just as they would have done 400 years ago."

Only, of course, it isn't just as they would have done. The modern Globe is connected to a modern building with running water, lavatories, bars, and cafés selling cellophane-wrapped sandwiches, hot tea and coffee, bottled beer, iced drinks. Electric lights shine and there are heaters. The audiences arrive in cars, or by bus or Underground. They very likely ordered an evening in this authentic Tudor playhouse by booking their seats on-line, with a plastic credit card. Sam Wanamaker's Olde Tudor Experience is about as authentically Tudor as Disney World.

The very idea of attempting to reconstruct the past, quite literally in this case, is an illusory and incidentally a very modern one. If we actually went back to the London of the sixteenth and seventeenth centuries we should find a largely wood-built, smelly, plague-ridden city bursting with a population explosion.

In 1500, there were about 75,000 Londoners. By 1600, there were around 200,000; by 1650, perhaps double that. This was in spite of the fact that plague was frequent. Indeed, the persistent recurrence of the disease makes it all the more remarkable that the late sixteenth century was a time when the English drama, properly speaking, began, for at every outbreak of the plague, the theaters closed and the actors and managers lost their income.

For example, consider the theatrical company known as Strange's Men, patronized by Ferdinando Stanley. Lord Strange (later Earl of Derby) performed "harey the vi" (*Henry VI*) to good audiences at Philip Henslowe's Rose Theatre on 3 March 1591–2. Henslowe made £3 from one performance, £3 16s 8d at another: this was big money. Thomas Nashe said that there had been "ten thousand spectators," but by June the theater had closed because of plague. Nashe—possibly an early collaborator of Shakespeare's—like with Marlowe, Greene, and Peele, always had to look about for some nondramatic work to bring in an income when the theater was closed; his pornographic poem "The Choice of Valentines" is an evocation of brothel life in Southwark in the 1590s. Strangely enough, the only fear haunting this poem, sometimes called "Nashe's dildo," is not of plague or venereal disease but of impotence.[1]

When one thinks of the fact that the inhabitants of Tudor and Stuart London all believed in hell, or supposedly did so, it is fascinating that they continued to indulge so freely in sexual vice of all kinds. Shakespeare's Sonnets, also written to keep the wolf from the door while the theaters were closed, reflects a bisexual world where abstinence is not even considered. When Shakespeare writes of the brothel in *Measure for Measure,* it is obvious that he writes from experience, and that he was not unusual. Henry VIII, in 1546, had ordered the closure of all the stews in Southwark. This was a bit ripe, coming from a monarch who was himself riddled with syphilis, and after his death the following year, under the kingship of his Puritan young son Edward VI, the bordellos reopened.[2]

The first great historian of London, John Stow, lived from 1525—he was born in the parish of St. Michael Cornhill, the son of a tailor—to 1605. He was over sixty when the first edition of his great book was published in 1598, but he had given his whole life to the *Survey of London.*

Stow was an intensely conservative and pessimistic observer of the London scene. He told a friend towards the end of his life that he had talked as a youth with old men who remembered Richard III as a comely prince.[3] He had a passion for details—the beauty of a perished bell tower in Clerkenwell, the decoration of the old Blackwell Hall. He saw London as being steadily wrecked by overpopulation, overbuilding, and the greed of developers, City men, and speculators. Every monument, every parish record had been perused by Stow. He was as fond of his recollections of the sedgy ditches near Moorgate as he was of the old stocks by Walbrook. Now he saw only swindlers "that more regarded their own private gain than the common good of the city."

Stow had lived through an extraordinary century. While he was in his twenties, more than two hundred Protestants were burnt alive for heresy at Smithfield Market between 1554 and 1558 under the religious fanaticism of Mary Tudor. These times were followed by Elizabeth I's spy ring and its attempt to round up Catholic dissidents—"the fools of time," Shakespeare called them, "Who died for goodness who had lived for crime." For the Elizabethans, Roman Catholics, with their willingness to plot against the Queen and use violence in the furtherance of their ends, occupied something of the same position that Muslims have in the modern world. They were objects of suspicion, and it was felt that their uncompromising religious views were incompatible with good citizenship. Stow had an equal horror of the Puritan sectaries, whom he saw as spoiling the sensible church-state balance that was the Elizabethan Settlement.

You see the power of ideas to move and to change human beings if you follow the life career of another Londoner, who was born three years after Stow's death, in Bread Street, the son of a scrivener. John Milton grew up in the very same street that contained the Mermaid Tavern, one of the favorite drinking places of Ben Jonson and Shakespeare. (It was owned by the Fishmongers' Company.)

> What things have we seen
> Done at the Mermaid!

exclaimed their fellow to dramatist Beaumont,

> Heard words that have been
> So nimble, and so full of subtle flame,
> As if that every one from whence they came
> Had meant to put his whole wit in a jest,
> And had resolved to live a fool the rest
> Of his dull life.

The boy Milton—a "pigeon of Powles," as the pupils at St. Paul's School were called—would have heard the drunken laughter of these elder poets drifting up from the street as he damaged his eyes reading late into the night. He stayed in London throughout his life, seeing the Civil War and seeing the monarchy out.

Milton had been the keenest and most articulate supporter of the English revolution. He did not sign the death warrant for the King, but he worked as Latin Secretary to Oliver Cromwell; this, the equivalent of being foreign secretary, entailed writing letters to foreign powers on behalf of the new English republic and welcoming their embassies and delegations. English republicanism was very much a product of the

Puritanism which flourished in the City of London, and it modeled itself very much on that of the Dutch.

Charles I, the most aesthetically intelligent of all English monarchs, had looked at the models of Italy and France to re-design his London. He was able to employ the services of Inigo Jones (1573–1652), son of a cloth worker from St. Benet, Paul's Wharf. The architect, who had made a deep study of Palladio, did stage design for masques and plays by Ben Jonson. (Jonson gracelessly thanked him by caricaturing Jones as "the joiner of Islington" in *A Tale of a Tub*.)

Jones wanted to make London as beautiful as Paris or Venice. He laid out Covent Garden in the Earl of Bedford's estates with arcaded piazzas modeled on the Place des Vosges (Place Royale, as it was in those days). As Surveyor General of the King's Works, he built the Queen's House in Greenwich and laid out the grandiose Whitehall. The only surviving Jones building in Whitehall is the Banqueting House, completed in 1622. The ceiling is filled by Rubens paintings placed there by the discerning Charles I in the 1630s. Little can he have known that Inigo Jones, that great designer of pageants and stage shows, had provided in the Banqueting Hall a background like none other for the most dramatic end to any royal drama.

After a trial in Westminster Hall, the King was condemned to death, and the execution took place on January 30, 1649. A scaffold was erected outside the Banqueting House, to avoid the necessity of conducting the King to Tower Hill (the normal place for public executions) and risking public disorder. Almost the last sight the King would have had, as he walked through the hall, would have been the great Rubens ceilings. He stepped out of the window onto the scaffold, Bishop Juxon accompanying him. It was one of the most extraordinary moments in English history, silent, cold. None of the crowds could hear his dignified last speech. He was too far away from them. As he knelt, his final word was "Remember." A light falling of snow scattered the crowd as the ax fell. One eyewitness said that "there was such a dismal groan among the thousands of people that were within sight of it (as it were WITH ONE CONSENT) as he had never heard before."

6

RESTORATION

Paris remains a city divided by the revolution of 1789. In all its subsequent great crises—in 1848, in 1870, in 1940—the old fissures open; the wound still bleeds. London, which had been a republican stronghold during the English revolution, welcomed the return of a monarchy whose power was restricted by that of an aristocratic oligarchy, and of the City itself. Charles II, a canny and affable monarch, was personally responsible for putting the past of the revolution behind him and letting bygones be bygones. Reprisals against those who had supported the execution of his father were few, and Pepys's well-known account of the execution of one of the regicides, Major-General Harrison, captures the spirit of London at the time, a London determined to put the past behind it and concentrate on present business:

October 13 1660:

To my Lord's in the morning, where I met with Captain Cuttance. But my Lord not being up, I went out to Charing-Cross to see Major-General Harrison being hanged, drawn and quartered—which was done there—he looking as cheerfully as any man could do in that condition. He was presently cut down and his head and heart shown to the people, at which there was great shouts of joy. It is said that he said he was sure to come to the right hand of Christ to judge them that have now judged him. And that his wife doth expect his coming again.

Thus it was my chance to see the King beheaded at White-hall and to see the first blood shed in revenge for the blood of the King at Charing-Cross. From thence, to my Lord's and took Captain Cuttance and Mr Sheply to the Sun taverne and did give them some oysters. After that I went by water home, where I was angry with my wife for her things lying about, and in my passion kicked the little fine Baskett which I bought her in Holland and broke it, which troubled me after I had done it. Within all afternoon, setting up shelves in my study. At night to bed.

Apart from the callous sublimity of Pepys himself, this passage brings home to us the quite extraordinary peacefulness of the counterrevolution. The King "enjoyed his own again" on May 29. The first blood shed against his former enemies was nearly five months later. Compare this with the blood in the Parisian gutters in 1870 or 1944.

The prosperity of the new order depended upon a king who was financed by the City, and on a growing capitalist class, a bourgeoisie, that was protected by a stable political system. London was at the very center of this political compromise. London in every sense underwrote it—in Westminster in its Parliaments, in the City by its ever burgeoning wealth. When, after the death of Charles II, his brother James II unwisely attempted to establish an absolutist and Catholic form of monarchy on a Continental pattern, there was no doubt where power actually lay. The bloodless revolution of 1688–89, and the replacement of James by the biddable Protestant William of Orange and his Stuart wife, Mary, only confirmed what had taken place at the Restoration of Charles II, namely a new form of monarchy, a new form of government.

In 1666, the Great Fire destroyed medieval London, its wooden houses, its alleys, its churches. The great Gothic cathedral of St. Paul's, restored in the time of Inigo Jones, had become woefully dilapidated in the intervening years. Dr. Christopher Wren, scientist-architect, had reported, two years before the fire, on the "ruin" of the roof and the "bending of the pillars." The fire reduced the cathedral to a shell. John Evelyn, on September 7, 1666, noted,

> It was astonishing to see what immense stones the heat had in a measure calcined, so that all the monuments, columns, friezes, capitals, and projections of massy Portland stone, flew off even to the very roof, where a sheet of lead (covering a great space no less than six acres by measure) was totally melted.... Thus lay in ashes that most venerable church, one of the most ancient pieces of early piety in the Christian world, besides near one hundred more.

The descriptions by Samuel Pepys of the fire itself are unforgettable: of the pigeons, flying with singed wings, or actually on fire, from their cherished eaves; of sick people carried out of houses in their beds; of the desperate urge to save property, some people piling their belongings into churches, or hurling them into the river to escape the flames; of the bridge forming a great arch of fire; of the panic-stricken crowds running, pulling carts, of the "horrid" "dreadfull" sky lit up at night; of oil cellars and brimstone bubbling and burning; of a cat, still alive, taken out of a hole in the wall of the Exchange with all its fur burnt away; of glass windows in houses and churches buckled and melted.

All this destruction provided Londoners with the chance to rebuild their city. Four hundred acres within the City walls and sixty-three acres outside them had been affected by the fire. Eighty-seven churches, forty-four livery halls, 13,200 houses, the Royal Exchange, the Guildhall were all partially or totally destroyed. Amazingly, only nine human lives were lost.

It is apt that the Monument, a tall column surmounted with a golden orb of flame, built in 1671–77 to commemorate the Great Fire and the rebuilding of the City that followed, should itself be a scientific instrument and contain the laboratory of one of the great scientists of the age.

Robert Hooke (1635–1703), astronomer, inventor of scientific instruments, speculative physicist, was one of the founder members of the Royal Society, that group of learned, chiefly Oxford, men, who had met during the Cromwellian years to discuss all aspects of learning, philosophy, and science. During the Protectorate they were centered on Wadham College, Oxford, but after the Restoration they made London their center and the King their patron. In November 1660, Charles II granted them their charter. The Royal Society still exists, the oldest scientific society in the world.

Hooke was a collaborator with Robert Boyle (1627–91) on his air pump, and his theoretical work on the weight, elasticity, and compressibility of air. Boyle's law (that the pressure of a given mass of an ideal gas is inversely proportional to its volume at a constant temperature) is only one of the many scientific insights brought to the world by the founders of this London-based institution. All the great scientists and innovators of this period were royalists, all were religious—Boyle was a keen theologian, who knew Hebrew, Syriac, and Chaldee, as well as Latin and Greek—and all were pious members of the Church of England.

Isaac Newton (1642–1727) was a keen and active member of the Royal Society, always making the journey from Cambridge to attend its meetings, and ending as its president. Newton's is not a specifically London story, but it is worth noting that here he was, a Cambridge genius among the older Oxford men, in London. This was the place where it seemed apt to share with the world his world-changing and prodigious discoveries, about optics, about the foundations and principles of mathematics, about gravity and astronomy, and, ultimately, about the nature of existence itself. Newton, infinitely the greatest scientific thinker ever born in Britain, felt it natural to gravitate to London to disseminate his learning and it was in the new London, rebuilt after the fire, that the new spirit could be embodied.

It is of these things that we think when we see the Monument to the Fire, with its underground laboratory and, at the top, its astronomical observatory. It was always intended by Hooke and the other members of the Royal Society as a place of scientific experiment as well as being, at 202 feet, the tallest isolated stone column in the world.

Its chief architect was Hooke's fellow scientist in the Royal Society, fellow Anglican, fellow son of the clergy, Christopher Wren. It was highly characteristic of the differences between the two men that Wren wanted the Monument to be crowned with a statue of Charles II and Hooke overruled him. Instead, Fire itself, that mysterious and destructive element, throws its gilt bronze flames into the London sky. The enormous cost of the Monument—£13,450 11s 9d—was borne by the Corporation of London.

To this day, the Square Mile of the City, London's financial capital, contains no Roman Catholic church. The Monument originally bore an inscription that spoke, in Latin, of the Fire and the damage it had caused. In 1681, however, were added the words "But Popish frenzy which wrought such horrors, is not yet quenched." There is no evidence that the Fire was the result of arson, still less of Catholic arsonists, but prejudice is as hard to quench as fire. Rather as, today, there is a link in public consciousness between Islam and terrorism, so, in seventeenth-century London, with its memory of November 5, 1605, when the plot to blow up Parliament was foiled, it was easy to identify Catholics with destruction. The insulting anti-Catholic inscription on the Monument was removed in

1831, two years after Parliament deemed it safe to allow Catholics to attend university, practice at the bar, and enter Parliament.

London's insularity, its paranoia, its unwillingness to absorb foreign or alien elements goes hand in hand with its sense of itself as modern and new. There is much in modern London that reflects this duality, this divided self-perception—in relation both to immigrants and to the question of whether Britain should be "part of Europe." Alexander Pope, himself a Catholic, alluded to the inscription on the Monument with the couplet

> Where London's column pointing at the skies,
> Like a tall bully, lifts the head, and lies.

Much of London's strength has been a bully's strength. Much of its beauty, certainly until the Second World War, was the creation of one man—Christopher Wren. When he died aged ninety-one, in 1723, his successor as architect in charge of St. Paul's Cathedral caused to be placed over the choir the inscription "Si monumentum requiris, circumspice" ("If you want to see his monument, look around"). Wren's full monument is not completed simply by looking around St. Paul's Cathedral. It is the whole of rebuilt London which is his monument—the fifty-two churches, the reconstructed and enlarged Temple Bar, the thirty-six company halls restored or rebuilt, as well as the two great hospitals for retired or injured servicemen: the Royal Chelsea Hospital (1689–92) for soldiers, and the Greenwich Royal Hospital (1699–1703) for retired and disabled seamen. In addition to the plenitude of magnificent and varied buildings must be considered Wren's part in advising the King and Corporation about the whole restructuring of London after the Fire. A commission was set up, with Wren himself,

Hugh May and Roger Pratt, Robert Hooke, Edward Jerman, and Peter Mills (the City surveyor). The first Rebuilding Act passed through Parliament on February 8, 1667. It laid down specific guidelines for the design of suitable houses, their height, the building materials, and the width of streets and guttering. The Act was less draconian than either Hooke or Wren would have wished, but one of the characteristics of London has always been its degree of architectural anarchy, the fact that it has never submitted itself to a single overall plan or planner.

A new Act was passed by 1670, to ensure that building regulations were being obeyed and that freeholders who lost property by street widening or the creation of new markets would be adequately compensated. By the 1667 Act, the City Corporation itself was granted the right to levy tax on imports coming into the docks. Coal, for example, was taxed at a shilling per ton, and this was tripled in 1670. The revenue from these taxes helped to finance the truly stupendous rebuilding program.

Wren is rightly remembered as a church builder, but he also built theaters, and this fact speaks volumes about the changes brought to London by the Restoration. The Rome of Bernini, the Paris of Le Nôtre were to have an English equivalent, with opera houses and theaters of a comparable style. The Theatre Royal, Drury Lane (1674) was one of Wren's great buildings. Such, indeed, was the extent of theater building in Restoration London that even in the heyday of Garrick, a century later, almost no new theaters needed to be built. The generation of Wren had done it for them.

After the period of the Protectorate, during which theater had been banned altogether, Londoners flocked to hear the old plays of Shakespeare, Ben Jonson, and their contemporaries. Pepys was typical in his enthusiasm. Like the architecture of the new theaters, the sets and scenery were works of art and immensely costly. In one of the many places known as Theatre Royal, that of Bridges Street, the actor-manager Killigrew (whose plays had gone on being surreptitiously performed in Cromwellian times) splashed out with amazingly elaborate scenery. Isaac Fuller took six weeks to paint the sets for Dryden's *Tyrannic Love*. The vast cost was recouped. In an extraordinary two-week run (most plays were only put on for a day or two) they took £100 per day at the box office, compared with usual receipts of £40 or £50. On February 5, 1664, Sir Robert Howard saw Dryden's *Indian Queen* and noted it was "so beautified with rich Scenes as the like had never ben seene here as happly (except rarely any where else) on a mercenarie theatre."

Restoration theater differed markedly from the old Elizabethan-Jacobean traditions. For a start, women for the first time in English history took to the boards. The second great difference is that the new theaters were entirely roofed in— there was no open space for the groundlings to stand. Audiences were ranged in social hierarchy, with the upper galleries, according to *The Country Gentleman's Vade Mecum* of 1699, full of servants; the middle gallery containing "the citizens' wives and daughters together with the Abigails, serving-men, journey-men and apprentices," and the pit reserved for "judges, wits and censurers... in common with those sit the squires, sharpers, beaus, bullies and whores and here and there an extravagant male and female sit." Even the upper gallery cost a shilling for admission, much more expensive than the penny charged to stand in the yard of Shakespeare's Globe.

Inevitably, Puritans found much to displease them about the revival of the theaters, nests of extravagance and license as they were. Many of the plays written by the new dramatists were risqué or absurd or both. The second Earl of Rochester (1648–80) set out to be shocking, and he embodied in his lyrics, many of them sung in the new theaters, all that the old Puritans found offensive:

> I rise at eleven, I dine about Two,
> I get drunk before Seven, and the next Thing I do
> I send for my Whore, when for fear of a *Clap*
> I dally about her and spew in her Lap.

In his retirement in Bunhill Fields, off the City Road, the blind republican John Milton meditated upon the tragedy of Samson, his eyes put out, pulling down the gaudy pillars of the Philistine theater and killing "Lords, ladies, captains, counsellors or priests," a scene which more vividly recalls the London theater land of the 1660s and 1670s than it does Gaza in the Bronze Age.

Yet, though Milton deplored the oafs and "hooray Henrys" in the streets—"the sons of Belial full of insolence and wine"—visitors to the London of the Restoration, and to the London that was rebuilt in the decades after the Fire, are more likely to have been struck by the business and hard work going on all around, than by the dissolute behavior of the few.

Imagine yourself, on a December day in 1711, walking through Temple Bar in the Strand and up Ludgate Hill. Towering above you is the newly completed dome of St. Paul's, a design which has all the baroque magnificence of one of the mightiest Roman churches, but that at the same time is mysteriously contained within a domestic scale. Do not let us enter the Cathedral, since, of all Wren's buildings, it has the most disappointing interior. Let us rather climb the hill towards it, and then look about us in the winter air and see the well-proportioned brick-built streets, with their pediments of Portland stone; see the company halls, a whole variety of styles, ranging from medieval Gothic to contemporary Baroque, but all achieving what a much later architect called "unity by inclusion." See the new Guildhall, reconstructed by Wren out of the ruins of the great medieval hall. (George Dance would make even greater improvements to the courtyard in 1789 with a playful Gothic all his own.)

See the quite extraordinary variety and ingenuity of Wren's fifty-one churches! The splendidly coffered dome of St. Stephen Walbrook mothers a quiet, pillared interior of extraordinary spiritual calm. The clear light of the windows in St. James Garlickhythe falls on what is in effect a quadrangle of free-standing columns, as if the mathematical genius of the Royal Society is contemplating the numerology of angels or the mathematical mystery of God himself. St. Lawrence Jewry, grand and pilastered, glows with gilded civic splendor, reflecting the wealth and self-confidence of the City merchants and burghers who have prayed there from its beginning. And here is St. Mary's Aldermary—one of Wren's Gothic surprises, a Perpendicular church of the fifteenth century, it seems at first when you step inside, but somehow, with its wide proportions, its great carved pulpit, and its sumptuous door case, very clearly an Anglican church from the heyday of Anglicanism.

No wonder that convert to Anglicanism T. S. Eliot so loved the City churches of Wren as he thought of

> where the walls
> Of Magnus Martyr hold
> Inexplicable splendour of Ionian white and gold.

For, like *The Booke of Common Prayer,* which was revised and restored for public use in 1662, these churches of Wren's (son of the royalist Dean) reflect a dignified but exuberant faith in the national Church. If anyone wanted to know what the true spirit of Anglicanism was, they would do better, rather than reading a book, to sit in one of these City churches, staring perhaps at a wooden reredos carved by Grinling Gibbons, with the Lord's Prayer and the Ten Commandments beside the Holy Table. They are both like, and utterly unlike, the continental Baroque churches of the period. Each has its own distinctive feel, yet all have in common an atmosphere of calm and strength. Outside, in the London that Wren had built, their steeples and towers and cupolas defined the skyline for three hundred years, and filled the London air with the music of their bells.

James II, who succeeded his brother Charles II in 1685, was a convert to Roman Catholicism; he attempted to follow the path of Mary Tudor 130 years earlier and take his kingdom back into the fold of European Catholicism. In the West Country, Charles II's illegitimate son the Duke of Monmouth led a rebellion, which was ruthlessly suppressed. The trials of Monmouth's supporters, condemned to death by the implacable Judge Jeffreys, were known as the Bloody Assizes. Monmouth himself was brought to London. At the age of thirty-six, he was beheaded on Tower Hill on July 15, 1685. His end was not the example of perfect Anglican piety that his friends the bishops had wished. Himself the son of Charles II's more promiscuous mistress, Lucy Walters, he was no stranger to the Tower of London. When he was a child of seven, he and his mother had been imprisoned there by Oliver Cromwell. He had watched her in turn be the mistress of several men before becoming a prostitute. It is perhaps not surprising that he was churlish towards his lawful wife even to the end, expressing on the scaffold his love for his adored Lady Wentworth. "God accept your repentance!" murmured the bishops, "God accept your imperfect repentance!"

The beheading itself was an example of English incompetence at its most terrible. Monmouth gave the axman six guineas before he died: "Here are six guineas for you. Do not hack me as you did my Lord Russell." He might have been tipping the barber. "I shall say little," he added in a loud voice, addressing the crowds that had assembled on Tower Hill to see the spectacle. "I come here not to speak but to die. I die a Protestant of the Church of England."

John Ketch then set to work with his ax. The first blow merely wounded him, and Monmouth rose from the block with a reproachful expression before collapsing. There was another stroke, and then another, but still the head had not come off. The crowds were by now enraged, and Ketch flung down the ax in nervous anger. "I cannot do it, my heart fails me."

"Take up the ax, man," said the sheriff of the City.

"Fling him over the rails!" shouted the crowd. There was now a danger that the mob would come and tear the executioner in pieces. Two more blows of the ax were still insufficient to remove the head, which like some idiocy by a butcher's apprentice had to be finished off with a sharp knife. The crowds then rushed forward to dip their handkerchiefs in the blood of a Protestant martyr.

James II, who was as clumsy in his management of public relations as John Ketch was with his ax, then contrived to pick a public quarrel with the bishops of the Church. His Declarations of Indulgence, which he commanded to be read in churches, were pleas of toleration for Christians of all faiths, Protestant and Roman Catholic. The bishops of the established Church saw them as an unsubtle attempt to destroy their very raison d'être. For them the Church of England was precisely that: the national Church, Catholic yet reformed, which made rival Protestantisms and rival Catholicisms an irrelevance. The King demanded that his bishops sign this Declaration; seven refused. In so doing, they achieved instant iconic status, particularly among the Protestant population of London. The Bishop of London, Henry Compton, was one of the celebrated seven; he had actually signed a petition already to William, Prince of Orange, to accept the throne of

England in James II's stead. The others were Archbishop Sancroft of Canterbury; Turner of Ely; Lake of Chichester; White of Peterborough; the saintly Bishop Ken of Bath and Wells; and Trelawney of Bristol. Upon their refusal to sign, and the King's insistence that they should do so, they were prosecuted for seditious libel and sent by boat to the Tower of London, crowds cheering them all the way. The churches of London were packed during their trial. The situation was seen by the London crowds, regardless of their enthusiasm for bishops, as a straight choice between the liberty of England versus the interference of Europe, Rome, and European-style Catholic despotism.

"We have two duties to perform," answered Bishop Ken when accused by the King of disloyalty. "Our duty to God, and our duty to your Majesty. We honour you, but we fear God."

Never before or since has a mob in England come out in favor of bishops, but James II managed to achieve this feat. They remained a week in custody, occupying the chapel of the Tower (which the King had set aside for Catholic worship) and reading the Anglican services. On June 15, the first day of the Trinity term, they were brought before the King's bench. A huge crowd followed them, which they blessed. Trelawney of Bristol, head of a great Cornish dynasty, inspired the ballad sung on a march on the capital from the West Country:

And shall Trelawney die, and shall Trelawney die?
Here's thirty thousand Cornish boys will know the reason why!

The bishops crossed the whole of London and were tried in Westminster Hall. Even the soldiers guarding them burst into cheering and applause when they were acquitted. James II, waiting at Hounslow for the news, heard the troops there burst into cheering. When he asked the cause he was told, "It is nothing—the Bishops have been acquitted."

"Do you call that nothing? *Tant pis pour eux, tant pis pour eux*": So much the worse for them.

In fact, as he must have realized at once, the spontaneous reaction of the London crowds to the trial and acquittal of the bishops was the surest possible indication that his experiment in Catholic absolutism had failed. It was not long before, that autumn, he left his kingdom. William of Orange arrived at Torbay in November and the bloodless revolution had been achieved. England was henceforth to be a country governed by a Protestant, Whiggish aristocracy, with the monarch as figurehead. It was very much part of this new deal that the monarch could, if necessary, be dismissed. And an essential feature of the whole new constitution was that it was supported and bankrolled by the very City merchants and money men who, in a previous generation, had so implacable a republican bias.

This is the era of the beginning of banking. During the Great Fire of 1666, Pepys anxiously buried his gold coins and valuables. In common with most Londoners, he kept his wealth at home in locked chests. In June 1667, when the Dutch fleet sailed up the Thames and there was a threatened invasion, Pepys sent his wife and servants into the country with as much gold as they could carry, some £2,300 worth, and kept another £300 hung from a girdle around his waist. He did not entrust his gold to the goldsmiths for safekeeping, as hundreds of other Londoners chose to do. Backwell the goldsmith had over half a million pounds on deposit from a thousand customers in September 1664. Scriveners (such as John Milton's father had been) would also hold deposits. Morris and Clayton held one and a half million in the 1660s. The vastly rich East India Company offered interest-bearing security and loans to favored clients.

Sir Francis Child (1642–1713) was a goldsmith, pawnbroker, alderman, and Lord Mayor of London, and by the 1690s he was concentrating exclusively on his banking activities. By the 1720s there were thirteen banks, mostly dealing with the great aristocratic families and largely located in the area of Fleet Street. (Child's Bank in Fleet Street closed only a few years ago.) Herries Bank in St. James's would advance loans to young aristocrats to pay for the Grand Tour. Hoares, Cootes, and Goslings were among the others. It was they, together with the East India Company, who underwrote payment for the army and navy. Edward, first earl of Clarendon, the historian of the English revolution and the father-in-law of James II, wrote that

> the bankers did not consist of above the number of five or six men, some whereof were aldermen and had been Lord Mayors of London.... They were a tribe that had risen and grown up in Cromwell's time, and never heard of before the late troubles, till when the whole trade of money had passed through the hands of scriveners: they were for the most part goldsmiths, men known to be so rich, and of so good reputation, that all the money of the kingdom would be trusted or deposited in their hands.

This is scarcely an exaggeration. Charles II "always treated these men very graciously," as well he might. His wars, his building plans, his new and efficient navy, his theaters and his churches did not come free. They were supplied to him, and to his successors, by the tribe that had risen up in Cromwell's time. It was now almost true that all the money in the kingdom was deposited in London. While the Treasury remained in Westminster, the institution that guaranteed national solvency was evolving in the City, eventually to be established formally as the Bank of England.

7

GEORGIAN

The late seventeenth century is the beginning of the story of modern London not merely because London was Britain's biggest port, handling 69 percent of total exports, 80 percent of all imports, and 86 percent of reexports. It was making itself unique in the world, because of what was happening in the City. But capitalism was never without its disasters as well as its triumphs.

In the third number of *The Spectator*, Saturday March 3 1710–11, the anonymous author (Joseph Addison) rambles into "the great hall where the bank is kept and was not a little pleased to see the directors, secretaries and clerks, with all the other members of that wealthy corporation, ranged in their several stations according to the parts they act in that regular and just economy." The congregation of City men are assembled to see "a beautiful virgin seated on a throne of gold. Her name (as they told me) was Public Credit."

The London of the early eighteenth century was the birthplace of modern banking and of the modern loan economy. Quite what money *is*—that is a question to which economists have never supplied a wholly satisfactory answer. But it is, among other things, the manifestation of power. What the brokers and bankers of early eighteenth century London did was to change money from a portable commodity—actual trunkfuls of gold (though it always was, and is, this too)—into the ability to promise and command payment: for city planning, for wars, for the running of the nation itself. It was the canny Chancellor of the Exchequer for William III, Charles Montagu, who, in the 1690s, effectively invented the Bank of England. The Bank came into being as a state lottery scheme, with two flotations in 1693 and 1694 raising £1.2 million from the punters. Henceforward, the country was run on credit and the national debt, so called, was of a scale that could never be paid off. This gave a quite unprecedented power to those— a tiny handful of bankers—who could control the supplies of money. The institution was called the Bank of England, but the directors of the bank and the money they commanded were in no sense nationalized. The directors were wheeler-dealers acting privately and hugely enriching themselves.

One of the many paradoxes about modern capitalism is that, while it was founded on the premise that the whole nation be placed in the debt of a few bankers, that private individuals should be in debt was considered profoundly wicked. In 1716, as many as sixty thousand debtors, some owing tiny amounts, were imprisoned in England and Wales. In London alone, between seven and eight hundred were imprisoned in the Marshalsea debtors' prison, of whom three hundred, in the single year of 1719, died of hunger.

The debtor government that allowed such fates to befall its debtor citizens ran into trouble by 1710. The governors of the Bank of England and the directors of the East India Company—the other body of financiers that bankrolled the government—were Whigs: that is, supporters of the Settlement of 1689, supporters of Dutch William, of Protestantism, and of a broadly antimonarchical government run by an alliance of aristocracy and City money. The new administration of Tories could not be sure that the City would go on underwriting their expenditure. Robert Harley became Chancellor of the Exchequer in 1710. There was a war with France to finance, and floating government debts of £9 million. An unsuccessful attempt to buy shares in the Bank of

England and stage a Tory takeover bid failed. Another company had to be found to finance government borrowing.

On September 10, 1711, that new company, formed by Harley, received the Royal Charter: the South Sea Company. Nine years later, this company, with investments of a sometimes nebulous character far away in the South Seas, had so many optimistic shareholders that it seemed to be in a position to take over the national debt itself. It was to take over £30 million of the debt (then standing at £51 million) in the first instance. With such a huge scheme in prospect, the South Sea Company found its shares dramatically rising. During 1720, they rose at a dizzying rate—130 percent in January, 1,000 percent in June. The prospect of watching savings multiply on such a scale was irresistible, and by now there were more than thirty thousand investors nationwide implicated in the fate of the company. After the increase of 1,000 percent, the overheated share price collapsed, falling from 780 percent to 180 percent by the end of June. By September the "South Sea Bubble" had burst and thousands of shareholders were ruined. "Work stopped on half-finished ships and partly-built houses.... Luxury trades, such as high-class tailoring, watches, plate, came almost to a standstill.... Unemployment and food riots were a serious possibility."[1]

The phantasmagoric nature of money and capital had been demonstrated to and by London, with life-shattering consequences. William Hogarth, the greatest English painter of the age, would in the 1730s depict the moral squalor of his times in the unforgettable series of "Progress" paintings, popularized in large-edition engravings—*A Harlot's Progress, A Rake's Progress,* and *Marriage à la Mode* (which was later, 1743–45)—all depicting a society whose values were utterly materialistic and selfish, and where the only consolations for the misery of a poverty-stricken life were to be sought in the taverns of Gin Lane or the arms of clap-ridden whores. In a sense the key to

Hogarth's whole oeuvre and outlooks, however, is to be found in a print he made in 1720 (when he was twenty-three years old), *An Emblematical Print on the South-Sea Scheme*. Beneath what looks like a parody of Wren's Monument to the Great Fire, money-mad speculators create their own conflagration and destruction on an infernal merry-go-round topped by the Golden Calf, on which apocalyptic horsemen ride.

Hogarth's was only one of many satirical responses to the Bubble. There was, for example, a set of playing cards with a mushrooming bogus company depicted on each one. Anti-Semites were not slow to observe that the radical change in the way that English fiscal and economic life was organized coincided with the arrival in the City of London of the Jews.

> Says a Rich Jew, to a Young Buxome Lady,
> I'll give you so much stock to let me Bed ye
> Quoth she you Lewd, Old Circumsiz'd Tom Cony
> I've Stock enough, I deal for ready Money.

In the period of the Protectorate, the Jews, who had been expelled from England during the Middle Ages, were invited back to reside in London. Menasseh ben Israel, resident in Amsterdam (though born in Madeira), was a theologian, an eloquent preacher, and a man of enormous personal charm. John Sadler, who met him in Amsterdam, described ben Israel as "a very learned Civil Man and a Lover of our Nation."[2] Another Puritan who met Menasseh ben Israel in 1652 wrote, "Lord, my heart questions not the calling home the nation of the Jews, thou wilt hasten it in thy season, oh my God." In October 1655 Menasseh ben Israel's petition "in behalf of the Jewish nation" called for the Jews to be allowed to return to London and live and worship freely. He wrote that he had "often perceived that in this nation [England] God hath a People, that is very tender-hearted, and well-wishing to our sore-afflicted Nation." The synagogue in Creechurch Lane does not survive, but that of Bevis Marks does; it has much the atmosphere of a Wren church, and it is easy to see why many English non-Jews thought of Judaism as a branch, in effect, of Protestantism.

Important as it was that the Jews of Amsterdam saw London as a place of tolerance, it is in some ways more important that they came from Amsterdam. The republican, newly emergent Dutch city had effectively invented modern capitalism—credit, insurance, banking. Menasseh ben Israel and his fellows brought Dutch skills, Dutch contacts, Dutch money to London. It is no surprise that the Dutch saw Cromwell's London as their greatest rival and threat, a view that led to three Anglo-Dutch wars: 1652–54; 1665–67; and 1672–74. In the second of these, the Dutch fleet sailed up the Medway and came close to a bombardment of London itself. It was the Dutch threat that led to the reorganization and building of the Royal Navy.

What the Dutch could see was that Britain had, in the East India Company, an outlet to Oriental trade that was fast outstripping all its rivals. In London, it had a port that was bigger and did more business than any other in Europe. And now, thanks to its contact with the money markets of Amsterdam, it had the makings of a modern financial institution.

The City of London, in all its medieval power structures, its Corporation, its companies based on medieval guilds and trades, its vast holdings of gold, its actual assets, had been badly shaken by the South Sea crisis. The City, in three subsequent centuries, would always see itself as the embodiment of probity and sound money. But what it had invented in the era of Wren was something that to an ungrateful world outside the Square Mile would often seem like a con, like money for nothing. From its beginnings the City, in all its august trappings and its amazing wealth, has had within it an element, not of dishonesty, but of conjuring, justifying the puzzlement of John

Maynard Keynes that the economy of the Western world could be run on the principles of the roulette wheel.

It is no surprise that one of the great heroes of the age was Jack Sheppard, robber, highwayman, and prodigious jail-breaker. His Houdini-like ability to extricate himself from handcuffs, leg irons, and chains, and to escape such fortresses as the Clerkenwell Bridewell, made him a hero. His emblematic importance in the scheme of things was recognized by the court painter and muralist James Thornhill, who came to paint him in his prison cell in Newgate. His hanging, which took place on November 16, 1724, was accompanied by huge crowds, as had been his trial in the Court of King's Bench, during which he told the judge, Justice Powis, that he had never had "the Opportunity to obtain Bread in an honest Way."

———

Jack Sheppard's body, as befitted a London hero's, was buried decently. The bodies of many hanged men and women, however, provided the raw material for another early-eighteenth-century obsession: dissection and anatomy. If the London of Wren and Hooke had led the world in chemistry and physics, then in the next generation the ancient medieval study of medicine was transformed into the modern science it is today.

Only the Barber-Surgeons' Company, the Royal College of Physicians, and the Royal Society were entitled to claim bodies for dissection. (In 1745, as a mark of its increasing distinction, the Surgeons' Company separated from the Barber-Surgeons.) The medical profession was moving up the social and intellectual scale. A body of men who in the seventeenth century had been functionaries wielding knives, some to shave and others to incise their clients, had divided, to form the Royal College of Surgeons.

To the old medieval foundations of St. Bartholomew's and St. Thomas's, private philanthropists added four new general hospitals: the Westminster (1720); Guy's (1725); St. George's (1733) for the East Enders in 1740; and the Middlesex (1745). It was also a period when specialized hospitals were established: three maternity hospitals in the middle years of the century; the Lock Hospital for venereal diseases in 1746; and the Foundling Hospital set up in 1739 by Captain Thomas Coram in Lamb's Conduit Fields, with its memorable murals by Hogarth of scriptural infants from Moses to Jesus.

Medicine was learnt in the London teaching hospitals. Students followed eminent surgeons and physicians on their ward rounds and paid for the privilege. In the mid-century a "walking pupil" would pay a surgeon between £21 and £32 a year, rather less to a physician. A dresser, one who helped with operations and performed minor bleeding, would pay £50 as an apprenticeship to an individual surgeon. This was a very lucrative business for the more distinguished doctors, and since everything in eighteenth-century London was measured by money it was the surest indicator of the doctor's change in status.

Much the most eminent anatomist of the eighteenth century was John Hunter (1728–93), who moved to London, having been a cabinetmaker's assistant in Glasgow, when he was twenty and who studied first at the Chelsea Military Hospital, then at St. Bartholomew's. Hunter, who experimented on fish, lizards, blackbirds, hedgehogs, and almost any creature he could lay hands upon to dissect, was a true scientist, an explorer of truth, a doubter. His axiom was that "experiments should not be often repeated which tend merely to establish a principle already known and admitted but that the next step should be the application of that principle to useful purposes." Dissection of corpses became, for him, more and more the means to establish a notion of the cause of disease.

But more was at stake than the mere analysis of spleen or liver or aorta. Hunter's lectures, published in the 1790s as

Philosophical Transactions, inevitably led some to question the existence of the soul. Hunter, a deist, had clung to the idea that there was a "vital principle," unseen but at work "in the blood and filth" discovered in the dissecting room. In a later generation, a major row broke out in the Royal College of Surgeons over this: Professor John Abernethy defended the vital principle against the materialistic rationalism of William Lawrence, who in a controversial lecture series in 1816 stated that there was no scientific evidence to suppose that such a principle existed. The blood and filth were all that there were.

———

Such a fear was merely heightened, not created, by the skills of anatomists. Religion seems to have coexisted with the most abject terror of death, which shudders through the life and writings of eighteenth-century London's most famous inhabitant, Samuel Johnson.

A penniless hulk of a man, he had "thought of trying his fortune in London" in 1737, when he was twenty-eight years old. He had lodged in the house of a staymaker in Exeter Street, off the Strand. Having earned his living more or less as a schoolmaster in the Midlands, he now set forth to be— what? A writer, a playwright, a Grub Street hack, eventually the celebrated dictionary maker and fount of conversational wisdom. The greatest of his contemporaries to make the change from provincial to metropolitan life, he was also emblematic of the trend that saw thousands do the same. Between 1700 and 1801, the population of the metropolis nearly doubled. It went from having 575,000 inhabitants to just less than a million.

In all its seething overcrowded darkened alleys and houses, hope for better things must have been nurtured—by thousands of Londoners who made it in trades and professions, and by thousands who would probably have been better off staying at home in their dull provincial towns and villages.

All Johnson's sayings about London, including the most famous, suggest the magnitude and comprehensiveness of what the place had to offer. "The world has nothing new to exhibit," he told the young Boswell, taking leave of the Scotsman over dinner at the Mitre Tavern in Fleet Street. "No man, fond of letters leaves London without regret." And "The happiness of London is not to be conceived but by those who have been in it. I will venture to say, there is more learning and science within the circumference of ten miles from where we now sit, than in all the rest of the kingdom." And "The town is my element." On September 20, 1777, when aged sixty-eight, he told Boswell: "You find no man, at all intellectual, who is willing to leave London. No, Sir, when a man is tired of London, he is tired of life; for there is in London all that life can afford."

Evidence of this life, the life of eighteenth-century London, remains in its surviving architecture, despite the ravages of Victorian builders, German aircraft, and twentieth-century developers and town planners. The first London square, Bloomsbury Square on the estate of Lord Southampton, had been laid out in the 1660s; Lord St. Albans imitated him a little later with the building of St. James's Square. But it was in the eighteenth century that the London square as a residential unit became so distinctive a feature, with regular terraces of houses enclosing a planted garden. Bedford Square of 1775, designed by Thomas Leverton; Cavendish Square, 1717, by John Prince; Portman Square, 1764; Manchester Square, 1776, are only some of them. Think of the stupendous Fitzroy Square, topped off with a magnificent Adam house in 1790, or of the Adam brothers' Portland Place, of 1778.

This was the age of some of the greatest London buildings, from Hawksmoor's (1661–1736) mysteriously original churches to William Kent's (1684–1748) old Treasury building and frontage to Horse Guards Parade, to Sir William

Chambers's (1726–96) Somerset House, and Albany in Piccadilly, to the varied achievements of George Dance the Younger (1741–1825). Witness the contrast between Dance's Gothic façade of the Guildhall in the City, of 1789, with the austerity of his (now demolished) Newgate Prison and the chaste simplicity of his terraced houses.

Though Londoners of the period lived cheek by jowl, many of them in abject poverty, none of them looked on anything that was visually ugly. The humblest tavern chair was well turned and chastely designed. The pewter or earthenware pot from which a poor man drank his ale had a simplicity of design that reflected the excellence of the apprentice system, by which craftsmen learnt over many years how to make things that were visually satisfying and physically useful. It was also, for the rich, the great age of furniture and china. Thomas Chippendale set up his workshop in St. Martin's Lane in 1753, working mainly in mahogany imported from South America; Thomas Sheraton followed in his footsteps in 1790 as the greatest furniture maker of the late eighteenth century and the Regency; Josiah Wedgwood manufactured his ceramics in Staffordshire but from early days had a London showroom, and Chelsea produced china in its way no less exquisite.

Nearly all the most beautiful silver in England now was made in London during the eighteenth century, many of the most beautiful clocks, the bindings on the most beautiful books. Nor was all this aesthetic achievement limited to the very rich or the privileged. A very distinctive and revealing feature of eighteenth-century life is the garden: not just the large public garden, laid out in the new-built squares, but behind the terraced houses space was reserved for small gardens. In an auction prospectus of March 12, 1802, a house at 53 Guilford Street, Queen Square, is sold on the strength of, among other things, "a large balcony overlooking the gardens of neighbouring dwellings." This has, ever since the reign of the first three Georges, been a feature of London life—that Londoners have been able to look out on their own back gardens and on the multifarious back gardens of others. "What a merry morning it is!" wrote Fanny Boscawen in May 1795, from her house at 14 South Audley Street. "I set all my windows open, and 'tis well I have some trees, whose leaves wave close by me, and that at once I behold purple lilacs, white lilacs, yellow laburnams [*sic*] in my own or my neighbour's garden." So there is a more than figurative truth in Johnson's words that "there is in London all that life can afford."

Consider that vast monument to the pleasures of talk, Boswell's *Life* of his hero, and the range and eminence of those with whom he held conversations, from King George III ("It was not for me to bandy civilities with my Sovereign") to the radical agitator Wilkes. Adam Smith, Edmund Burke, Edward Gibbon, Oliver Goldsmith, Sir Joshua Reynolds, Sheridan, Dr. Burney, Joseph Warton, innumerable bishops and peers all feasted on Johnson's conversation, as did his more intimate friends, who themselves embody the social mixture of Georgian London: Henry Thrale, the rich Southwark brewer, whose country house in Streatham provided such a refuge for Johnson and whose wife enjoyed an *amitié amoureuse* with the great wit; Frank Barber, the liberated West Indian slave who was to be Johnson's heir; Dr. Levett, the poor medic, evidently a drunk and a devoté of whores, who was one of Johnson's motley crew of lodgers in his various houses off Fleet Street and whose ministrations to the poor were celebrated in one of Johnson's finest poems. Think, too, of the vast variety of experiences recorded in Boswell, both in his life of Johnson and in his London journal. Eighteenth-century Londoners tended to live in small rooms and overcrowded houses. They took their social pleasures off home territory, as is witnessed by the popularity of pleasure gardens, coffeehouses, taverns, theaters.

By the late 1770s there were more than two hundred pleasure gardens in or around London. The two greatest were the Vauxhall Gardens, on the south bank of the river, and the Ranelagh Gardens (opened 1742), on the north bank in Chelsea. Parks have been an abiding refreshment to Londoners. Hyde Park was used for hunting deer until 1768. Since William III built Kensington Palace in the late seventeenth century, and Queen Caroline took the lease of the Dutch House at Kew in 1728, the parks have doubled as public and royal pleasure grounds. Kew was the place where in 1759 Augusta, Princess of Wales, established the Royal Botanic Gardens under the guidance of Lord Bute and his head gardener, William Aiton. It was embellished by superb temples, an orangery, and a pagoda by Sir William Chambers. (More wonderful buildings, including the hothouses, were designed a generation later by Decimus Burton.) But for the eighteenth century, apart from the horticultural pioneering done at Kew, parks were primarily places of recreation rather than of planting. It was the Victorians who first planted flowers, for example, in Hyde Park.

Roubilliac's statue of Handel in the Vauxhall Gardens (now preserved in the British Gallery in the Victoria and Albert Museum) is that almost of a minor god or sprite, whose presence provided a prodigious musical accompaniment to Georgian London life. Born in Lower Saxony, Handel was naturalized as an Englishman in 1727 and though his most famous oratorio had its first performance in Dublin (*Messiah*, April 13, 1742), nearly all the others were first performed in London, as were his numerous operas. His *Music for the Royal Fireworks* made him an apt *genius loci* for the pleasure gardens, since these places saw frequent pyrotechnic displays, as well as masques, dances, and theatrical extravaganzas. They were also, notoriously, excellent pick-up places, and casual sex was frequent in the darker walks away from the well-lit avenues.

Handel's move from composing mostly religious works, to be performed in church, to composing operas reflects the commercial importance of the theater to the London of the period. Some of the oratorios themselves, notably *Esther*, were actually staged. The Princess Royal wanted *Esther* to be put on at the King's Theatre in 1732 with scenery and action, but the Bishop of London intervened to prevent what was deemed a profanity (the acting out of a scriptural book, albeit a book that does not contain the word God).

There was money in theatrical work and Handel, who like most artists had his ups and downs, earned enough from his operas to be able to present the organ to the Foundling Hospital in 1750, with a performance of *Messiah* to celebrate the donation.

If Handel was well rewarded, then the most famous actor of the day was enriched beyond dreaming by the popularity of the London theater in the mid-eighteenth century. Garrick was primarily a comic actor—he made his first hit in a play called *The Lying Valet*—but he played most of the great Shakespearean roles and it is a debatable point whether he was a symptom or a cause of the enormous revival of Shakespeare's popularity at this time. It was as a manager that he enjoyed his greatest financial success. His productions ranged from the lavishly exotic—he thought nothing of hiring the greatest painters of his age, Zoffany and Reynolds, to paint his sets—to the imaginative and charitable. A pupil of Dr. Johnson, he always enjoyed an edgy relationship with his old master (Johnson resented his success), but one of the most magnanimous gestures ever devised by the two men was a charity performance of Milton's *Comus* at the Drury Lane Theatre in 1750, to raise money for Milton's granddaughter. She was the proprietor of a small greengrocery business in Holloway, and on the strength of the money raised she was able to move to the slightly more genteel suburb of Islington.

Theaters were not necessarily peaceful places. The audiences were often drunk and the price of admission charges was jealously watched. At a performance of Thomas Arne's opera *Artaxerxes* on February 24, 1763, it was discovered that the Covent Garden Theatre had charged more for tickets than its rival in Drury Lane. A riot broke out and so much damage was done that the theater had to be closed for several days.

Riot—that symptom of urban overcrowding and unease— was never far beneath the surface of Georgian London. In the 1760s, a petit bourgeoisie—small merchants, manufacturers, master craftsmen, shopkeepers: the very counterparts of those Parisians who would set in train the French Revolution twenty years later—rallied behind John Wilkes, the radical Member of Parliament for Middlesex, who called for their political enfranchisement with his campaign for adult male suffrage. The establishment badly misjudged the situation and the imprisonment of Wilkes for a supposed libel on the King inflamed his supporters. Rioters crying "Wilkes and Liberty!" clashed with the footguards in St. George's Fields, Southwark, in what was known (a few of them got killed) as the St. George's Fields Massacre.

Wilkes was in no modern sense left-wing. After his release from prison he became an immensely wealthy City merchant and a successful Lord Mayor in 1774. His immense popularity was not with those (like the Marxist revolutionaries of later periods) who would overthrow property, but rather with those who would see the indissoluble link between personal property and political freedoms. To that extent, the "Wilkes and Liberty!" riots foreshadowed the growth of the British bourgeoisie and the "liberal" economics of the nineteenth century.

But they also showed that London was a tinderbox politically, overcrowded as it was physically. In 1780, the British war against the American colonies was going badly, with depressing effect upon City trading and business generally. England's traditional old enemies, France and Spain, both joined forces with the Americans. There was nothing very Catholic about America in those early days, but the aggression of the French revived anti-Catholic prejudice in London. Some ill-timed parliamentary legislation, relaxing the outmoded penal laws against Catholics, was enough to spark the biggest riots London had ever seen. Lord George Gordon, leader of the Protestant Association, assembled a rally of sixty thousand supporters in St. George's Fields, the extensive open space between Southwark and Lambeth (long since built over) which had been the site of the "massacre" of April 1768. They marched across the Thames to present a petition to Parliament and then set to work torching various Catholic sites. The Bavarian embassy chapel in Warwick Street, the Sardinian embassy chapel in Lincoln's Inn Fields, and the mass houses in Moorfields were targets for the Protestant fanatics among the rioters. But, as a study of the rioters and their behavior shows, this was very far from being a simple piece of religious bigotry. Newgate Prison was attacked and set on fire and the prisoners released. Four other prisons were damaged. Lord Chief Justice Mansfield's house in Bloomsbury Square was attacked. We know a lot about the people who caused these arson attacks and about the people they set out to deliver. Newgate, for example, was successfully besieged by, among others, discontented sailors (cutlasses and marlin spikes were seen in some numbers among the crowds). The mob operated a frank protection racket. A Bishopsgate cheesemonger called Carter Daking was given the choice of paying money or watching his house go up in smoke: "Damn your eyes and limbs, put a shilling into my hat, or by God I have a party that can destroy your house presently."

This was not political discourse of a very elevated character. The Gordon Riots offered an opportunity for semi-articulated discontented malice to have its few nights of destroying, looting, burning, beating. The poor could show what they thought of the rich. The domestic servant could take it out on the well-established small shopkeeper. The drunken British oaf could show what he thought of the foreigners. Whereas the "Wilkes and Liberty!" riots had had a purpose, the Gordon Riots were more on the order of a primal scream. The attacks on Lord Mansfield's house, for example, were not merely a protest against the change of law to make life faintly easier for Catholics; they were an expression of loathing for a particularly unpopular Lord Chief Justice, during whose period of office the number of capital offenses was increased. At sessions presided over by Mansfield, 29 were sentenced to branding, 448 were transported, and 102 were hanged. For a man who sat as a judge in the Old Bailey perhaps once a year between 1757 and 1768 that was quite an impressive bag, and those deported, branded, and hanged would have had many friends and relations who would derive, no doubt, some pleasure from watching Mansfield's furniture and pictures burn while he and his wife slipped out the back door. The government was not going to allow the situation to turn from a riot into a revolution, however, and ten thousand troops were brought in to quell the disturbances. By the end of a week, two hundred had been killed, twenty-five were hanged, and an amazingly few buildings (fifty-odd) were found to have been damaged, giving credence to the idea that the targets were not random but chosen with premeditated care.

Insofar as they were a protest against the different, the foreign, the various, the Gordon Riots were only an extreme expression of a London phenomenon that repeats itself continually as the city expands and changes. The population growth of Georgian London was not caused by a prodigious increase in the fecundity of women born within the sound of Bow Bells. It was caused largely by those who came to London, as Johnson had done, to try their fortune.

Many came, like Johnson himself, from the provinces. Yet others came as a result of the huge increase of world trade centered upon the port of London—sailors, slaves and ex-slaves, mulattos and quadroons. Many blacks joined in the Gordon Riots: "The voice of our complaint implies a vengeance," said one who spoke for them, Ottobah Cugoano, famed in his day as a writer.

But the most significant immigrant community during this century was the French. They were almost all Huguenots (Protestants) escaping the religious intolerance of their native country; and though not exclusively responsible for the silk industry, which centered upon the district of Spitalfields, they were preeminent in it.

The great portraits by Thomas Gainsborough (1727–88) seem to be commentaries on the common proverb of the time—"We are all Adam's children, but silk makes the difference." The animated English faces of Gainsborough's women look at us from the top of extravagant festoons of silk, shimmering and cascading across the canvas. Gainsborough usually gives twenty times as much space to the silk dress as he does to the face of his sitter. The expense of silk and the sheer artistry of the dressmaking mark the sitters out from the generality of mankind, clad in wool and worsted. The average wage of a journeyman silk weaver might be five shillings per week. The price of a silk dress would be fifty pounds. It would take a weaver four years, in other words, to earn the price of such a dress. Lesser workers in the industry, winders and spinners, usually boys or women, might earn as little as a shilling a week.

Huge fortunes were made by the silk manufacturers themselves. By 1777 the bigger merchants, such as Vansommer and Paul of Pall Mall, were insuring their businesses for the prodigious sum of £21,000. By then, what is known as the Industrial Revolution was under way, and London was at its hub.

8

THE INDUSTRIAL REVOLUTION AND THE METROPOLIS OF NASH

Twentieth-century historians of the Industrial Revolution in Britain tended to overlook entirely, or grossly to underestimate, the central importance of London as a manufacturing and industrial base. "Not London, but Manchester, Birmingham, Leeds, Glasgow and innumerable small proletarian towns launched the new era" is a typical assessment, by Fernand Braudel. A study of facts, following the pioneering work by Roy Porter (*London: A Social History,* 1994) and Martin Daunton (*Progress and Poverty,* 1995), demonstrates the wrongness of this view.

The sheer size of London compared with the burgeoning industrial cities is the first factor that earlier historians overlooked in their effort to suggest that London's wealth came from trade and commerce while the rest of the country actually manufactured the goods. If we accept that by 1801 London had a population of 960,000, that makes it over ten times the size of Liverpool (82,000). Nor is it true, as earlier historians believed, that the population of London leveled off or declined. They took their statistics from those actually living within the City. There was huge overspill, with populations filling and urbanizing the villages of London. The population of Marylebone alone was 122,000 in 1831, larger than that of Leeds, whereas the parish of St. Pancras, adjoining it, contained a populace of 103,000, the size of Bristol.

All these people had the ambition, not always fulfilled, of eating on a daily basis. They all wanted, and many were gratified in their want, clothes, shoes, china, table linen, furniture, tobacco, garden shears, coal scuttles, carpets, watches and clocks, scissors, ointments, pills and potions, mattresses, leather pouches, books, baskets, wheelbarrows, candles and candle snuffers, dolls and dollhouses, carriages, wooden legs, spectacles, and the thousand and one objects with which urban people clutter their existence.

Some of these things were manufactured in other parts of the British Isles and purchased by Londoners. But all of them were also manufactured in London or its immediate environs, and the study of trade directories—most prominently the *London and Provincial New Commercial Directory* printed by Pigot and Company—itemizes 49,000 businesses, of which over 35 percent were engaged in manufacture of some kind. (This excludes bespoke production.)

Water was not something you readily drank in these unhygienic times. Beer was the usual drink for breakfast as well as for dinner, for children as for grown-ups. There were innumerable small brewers in Georgian London, and some very wealthy ones like Dr. Johnson's friend Henry Thrale. Whitbread's, Barclay's, and Truman's breweries accounted for nearly 36 percent of London's beer consumption by the early nineteenth century. This involved highly developed steam-operated technology, to provide the gallons of ale required to slake the capital's thirst.

London was also the national center of gin distilling. (Eight million gallons of gin were consumed annually by the British in 1745, and although this rate declined in the next sixty years, there were still seventy-five gin distillers in London at the turn of the eighteenth and nineteenth centuries.)

Sugar, imported directly from the West Indies into London docks, was refined in the capital; this was the third greatest food or drink manufactory. But until the twentieth century the vast population of London was largely self-sufficient in comestibles, with lard, oil, mustard, vinegar, chocolate, biscuits, and many other such everyday items being factory produced in the capital. Readers of Marx's *Das Kapital* will recall his haunting description of the grueling hours worked by bakers, and their average age of death—forty-two.

The industrial basis of London's wealth and the industrial complexion of Londoners' working lives are something of which we need to remind ourselves today, since they have all but vanished. In Camden Town, for example, a place where until the early to mid-twentieth century small factories produced pianos, gin, and artificial limbs, these have all been converted for office or domestic use.

In 1824, when he was twelve years old, Charles Dickens lodged in these parts while his father was incarcerated in the Marshalsea prison for debtors in Southwark. Every day the tiny boy walked down from his north London lodgings to a factory just off the Strand, which made paste blacking for boots and fire grates:

> The blacking warehouse was the last house on the left-hand side of the way, at Hungerford old-stairs. It was a crazy, tumble-down old house, abutting of course on the river, and literally over-run with rats. Its wainscotted rooms and its rotten floors and staircase, and the old grey rats swarming down in the cellars and the sound of their squeaking and scuffling coming up stairs at all times, and the dirt, and the decay of the place, rise up visibly before me as if I were there again. The counting-house was on the first floor, looking over the coal-barges and the river. There was a recess in it, in which I was to sit and work. My work was to cover the pots of paste-blacking; first with a piece of oil-paper; to tie them round with a string; and then to clip the paper close and neat, all round, until it looked as smart as a pot of ointment from an apothecary's shop. When a certain number of grosses of pots had attained this pitch of perfection, I was to paste on each a printed label; and then go on again with more pots.

The memory of the blacking warehouse was bitter. Dickens's friend and biographer John Forster knew nothing of it until he had known the writer well for some years and they happened to meet a Mr. Dilke, who remembered giving Dickens a half-crown when he was the little factory boy.

Dickens's earliest writings, which came out in the *Evening Chronicle,* were the *Sketches by Boz:* snapshots of London and Londoners in the mid-1830s, but drawing on memories which stretched right back to his lonely and frightening childhood when, often abandoned to his own devices or to the drudgery, near slavery, of the warehouse routines, he would wander the streets, taking in their sights, sounds, characters. Boz sees the condemned cell at Newgate, the Vauxhall Pleasure Gardens, theaters, offices, churches. We see the way that London fed his imagination as an artist, to the extent now that when we think of the early-nineteenth-century capital, we see it through his spectacles: whimsical, comical, pathetic, funny—in a word, Dickensian. Dickens captured London, made it his.

It is sometimes necessary, if we are as spellbound by Dickens as most English readers are, to remind ourselves that in the period between the Napoleonic Wars and the accession of Queen Victoria, London was more than the fogbound shabby-genteel clerk-infested world of soot-covered muffin men and sneezing beadles depicted by Boz. It was becoming the first major metropolis in the world. Its population was swelling: between the beginning of the nineteenth century and 1840, 865,000 people grew to 1.5 million. But more than mere population growth was taking place. London was not only the biggest city in the world. It was, after the Napoleonic wars, the one which dominated.

Knight's Cyclopaedia of London, 1851 noted:

Some years ago, in pulling down the French church in Threadneedle Street, there was exposed to view a tessellated [mosaic] pavement, which, at least fourteen centuries ago, had borne the actual tread of Roman feet; and the immediate neighborhood was probably the most opulent part of Roman London. A greater power than the Roman, a power of which the masters of the old world had no conception, now reigns supreme on this very spot.[1]

Backed by political domination of Europe and of India, by a formidable industrial base in its own metropolis and in Britain as a whole, and by that very system of credit which at the time of the South Sea Bubble had seemed so insubstantial and unsound, the commercial wealth of the City of London was the cornerstone of nineteenth-century London's wealth. Whereas the French had relied upon direct taxes, often deemed unfair, to raise revenues, the English, since the time of the setting up of the Bank of England and the national debt, had financed loans and investment as the basis of security and prosperity. When it worked, as in good times it did, investors were happy and the populace at large, by a sleight of hand, could go untaxed.

High finance has always had its hazards. The great loan contractors for the British wars against Napoleon were the Goldsmids. Aaron Goldsmid was a Dutch Jew who had settled in London in the mid-eighteenth century. Benjamin and Abraham Goldsmid became bill brokers. They remained in close contact with Amsterdam, still the major European money market. Benjamin, who secured a dowry of £100,000 on his merger with a prosperous East India merchant, Israel Solomons, became one of the great figures of the stock exchange, a financial adviser to William Pitt, and a key figure in the war against Napoleon. Both brothers, Benjamin and Abraham, committed suicide, Benjamin in 1808 and Abraham in 1810, having underwritten loans which could not be repaid as a result of crashes in the market. The family business was rescued by Asher

Goldsmid's son Isaac Lyon Goldsmid, who grew to be one of the greatest financiers in the City, and by an association with the Baring brothers. Francis Baring (1740–1810) was the grandson of a Lutheran minister from Bremen. From the first, the City of London had this cosmopolitan flavoring, and the success of its capital market was in large measure owing to its transcendence of petty national boundaries. None of the money, however, would have been made had there not been actual investments in manufactured or imported commodities that people needed or wanted to buy. The development of the docks and the construction of the enclosed docks in the City by William Jessup and Ralph Walker in the Isle of Dogs and by William Vaughan at Wapping, with separate basins for import and export, were vital in Britain's commercial success.[2]

Yet, for all its wealth and size, London, even as it emerged as the preeminent world capital, resisted the overall makeover that, for example, Paris would undergo, first in Napoleonic times, later in the era of Baron Haussmann, in which boulevards and avenues were forced into existence regardless of what houses, shops, or gardens lay in their way. The gentle sweep of John Nash's Regent Street tells its own story. Sir John Summerson (*Georgian London,* p. 168) says that "this great thoroughfare is unique in the history of town-planning. Its amazingly successful blend of formality and picturesque opportunism could have happened nowhere and at no time but in England of the period of the picturesque."

Its placing was determined by the inexpensive, higgledy-piggledy margins of Soho property to its easterly side and the expensive estates of Mayfair. Jo Mordaunt Crook complements Sir John Summerson's vision with his pithy observation that "the sinuous path of Regent Street was not Hogarth's line of beauty but the developer's line of maximum profit." Nash's original conception, shared with his royal patron the Prince Regent, had been a rebuilding of central London on a Parisian scale, with a grand central, straight boulevard, lined with monuments, stretching from Carlton House, the Prince's palatial residence on the edge of St. James's Park, to the newly designed Regent's Park in the north. New Street (as Regent Street was going to be called) would march on three axes, Piccadilly Circus, Oxford Circus, and Regent Circus, with a piazza and a huge colonnade. The cost would have been prohibitive and Nash and his patron had to wait for the lease to fall vacant on Crown land before constructing the compromise scheme.

At quite a late stage of the plan, All Souls' Church on Langham Place was designed and incorporated, part place of worship, part eyecatcher. The sweep of Regent Street looking northwards is enhanced by this graceful building with its pencil steeple; and there in the portico is the bust of John Nash, its architect and the overall inspiration of this New London. Many architects and designers helped to reshape Regency London—Smirke, Repton, Decimus Burton—but it is Nash who was the great town planner, and it is largely to Nash that we owe the beautiful creamy stuccoed grandeur of Portland Place, and to the north the rich varieties of architectural fantasy in Regent's Park, culminating at the top with the Zoological Gardens and his villas in Park Village East and Park Village West.

The London parks in the nineteenth century reflected the dawnings of democracy. As more and more people crowded into the metropolis, they felt ever more keenly the need for the "lungs" provided by parks. As well as places to stroll or hear music, the London parks became the people's gardens. In 1843, the *Gardener's Chronicle* remarked that "naming of trees and shrubs in Kensington Gardens as anticipated, has had a beneficial effect upon the public mind awaking a curiosity and a taste for botanical and horticultural pursuits so much so that gentlemen go straight from the gardens to the nurseries."[3]

Regent's Park, from its beginnings, after the falling in of a lease on farmland in 1811, was a place of horticultural, zoological, and visual delight for the public. When the Zoological Gardens opened in 1828, with buildings by Decimus Burton, they received thirty thousand visitors in the first seven months. The overall shape of the park, however, with its crescents, its inner circle, its shrubberies and walks, its boating lake and its mounds (simply created from the rubble caused by building the surrounding terraces), its refreshing illusions of "country in the town" (*rus in urbe*), were the inspiration of one man, John Nash.

It is to Nash that we owe the outline of the West End. The Prince Regent's residence, Carlton House, having had untold riches spent upon its extravagant gilded interiors, was demolished, and Nash rebuilt Buckingham House as a royal residence. The money was always running out for Nash with his grand schemes. His vast Waterloo Memorial never got built, but it was he who laid out Trafalgar Square. In its midst is London's best-known monument, Nelson's column, 170 feet of Devon granite, with a seventeen-foot bronze statue of the hero of Trafalgar at its top. The column is by William Railton and the statue by E. H. Baily. It is deeply significant that the British capital has at its emotional and touristic center a monument not to a politician or a dictator or a king, but to a great naval hero—and one, moreover, whose irregular private life hugely added to his popularity. This, says the monument, has never been a capital city ruled over by dictators. It is a mercantile and commercial capital, protected by Britain's independent island status.

At the top of Trafalgar Square, Nash at first thought to build a terrace of grand houses such as those in Regent's Park, but then came the brilliant idea of housing the collection of paintings belonging to the Russian merchant John Julius Angerstein, which had been bought for the nation by Sir

George Beaumont and King George IV. But the National Gallery by William Wilkins is dull, one of London's architectural failures, the dome too small, the proportions of the elevation facing the square, and the height, jarringly wrong.

The same could not be said of the British Museum, which had originated in the eighteenth century to house various collections, such as the King's library, Sir William Hamilton's collection of antique vases, and Charles Towneley's collection of antique sculpture. In 1816, Lord Elgin, at great cost and risk to himself, had rescued the marbles from the Parthenon in Athens where the Turkish ruling authorities had allowed them to languish into disrepair. (He ruined himself by the purchase of these friezes, though his name is often libeled by journalists who say that he stole them.) A building worthy of the Athenian masterpieces needed to be constructed; in Robert Smirke they found the perfect architect. The British Museum is as glorious as the National Gallery is undistinguished. (It was not until 1852–57 that the courtyard was converted to the circular reading room beloved of Thomas Carlyle, Karl Marx, and George Bernard Shaw.) The arrival of the Parthenon marbles, at a period of history when no such country as Greece existed, was one of the glory moments of the Greek Revival in London.

St. Pancras Parish Church by H. W. Inwood and W. Inwood, with its imposing caryatids overlooking the porch; Decimus Burton's Athenaeum Club, adorned with its frieze and its great gilded statue of the goddess Athene over the porch, and his Ionic screen at Hyde Park Corner; Smirke's Royal Mint; and Philip Hardwick's great arch at Euston Station (unforgivably demolished by British Rail in 1964)—these were among the great expressions of British Hellenism. When they looked back at Athens, a small city-state in the fourth century B.C., dominated by an oligarchy of bookish, intelligent men and protected by heroic soldiers and sailors, they saw a reflection of how they would like to view themselves. The center of London's wealth and the symbol of its independent status, the Bank of England itself, was rebuilt by Sir John Soane in his own highly distinctive, not to say eccentric, version of the Greek style, though we know its great interiors, its dome, and caryatids only from photographs since it was vandalistically rebuilt in 1925–39. (Soane's own house, however, survives as the Sir John Soane's Museum at Number 13 Lincoln's Inn Fields, one of the great monuments to human eccentricity that London can provide. Were I to show a tourist one thing in the capital, it would be this.)

The capital's first democratically elected mayor, Ken Livingstone, produced a huge plan for London in 2002. It must occupy some of our thoughts at the end of this short book. It offers promises that if London has problems, the mayor will, in one of his favorite verbs, "tackle" them. "Discrimination" and "deprivation" will vanish under democracy's benignant gaze, as it builds "a London that is more accessible to disabled people."

The London of John Nash and George IV, of the child Dickens and the old William Blake, was probably highly discriminatory, pitiless to the poor and the disabled, and unwilling or unable to "tackle" their problems. Blake saw its industrial mills as satanic and, wandering through its chartered streets "near where the chartered Thames does flow," he saw "marks of weakness, marks of woe" in the inhabitants. But it was also a time of magnificence and beauty, when London bubbled not only with riches but also with cleverness and brilliance. When Wordsworth, a year before noting that "earth hath not anything to shew more fair" than Westminster early in the morning, invited Charles Lamb to stay in the Lake District, Lamb replied:

> I don't much care if I never see a mountain in my life. I have passed all my days in London, until I have formed as many and intended local attachments as any of you mountaineers can have done with dead Nature. The lighted shops of the Strand

and Fleet Street; the innumerable trades, tradesmen, and customers, coaches, waggons, playhouses; all the bustle and wickedness round about Covent Garden; the very women of the Town; the watchmen, drunken scenes, rattles; life awake, if you are awake, at all hours of the night; the impossibility of being dull in Fleet Street; the crowds, the very dirt and mud, the sun shining upon houses and pavements, the print-shops, the old book-stalls, parsons cheapening books, coffee-houses, steams of soups coming from kitchens, the pantomimes—London itself a pantomime and a masquerade—all these things work themselves into my mind, and feed me without a power of satiating me.

If such pleasures were on offer to anyone who walked the streets with Lamb's attentive eyes and ears, the life in the houses of the rich and great was incomparable. Spencer House, overlooking Green Park and now open to the public, is the last great aristocratic house in London to survive. Holland House in the park of the name was destroyed by a bomb in the Second World War. It is hard to think of funnier, or more enviable, social gatherings than those attended by the young Thomas Babington Macaulay and old Samuel Rogers, the banker poet, at Holland House: "We breakfasted on very good coffee, and very good tea, and very good eggs, butter kept in the midst of ice, and hot rolls." The talk was often, by the 1830s, of figures from the Hollands' past. Amid all the wit and laughter, the puns and verbal games, the portraits by Lawrence looked down on a group of people who were becoming obsolete. Byron, Sir Walter Scott, and Charles James Fox were remembered, but a different world was dawning. And by the time Queen Victoria came to the throne in 1837, it had definitely begun.

9

VICTORIAN LONDON

In *Dombey and Son* there is an unforgettable description of the devastation brought to Camden Town by the coming of the railways:

> The first shock of a great earthquake had, just at that period, rent the whole neighbourhood to its centre. Traces of its course were visible on every side. Houses were knocked down; streets broken through and stopped; deep pits and trenches dug in the ground; enormous heaps of earth and clay thrown up; buildings that were undermined and shaking propped by great beams of wood....
>
> Everywhere were bridges that led nowhere; thoroughfares that were wholly impassable; Babel towers of chimneys, wanting half their height; temporary wooden houses and enclosures, in the most unlikely situations; carcases of ragged tenements, and fragments of unfinished walls and arches, and piles of scaffolding and wilderness of bricks, and giant forms of cranes, and tripods straddling above nothing.

It does not take much imagination or detective work, as you walk round London in the twenty-first century, to see how much of it was built during the reign of Queen Victoria—from its Gothic Houses of Parliament by Charles Barry (and exotically furnished and decorated by Augustus Welby Pugin) spreading outwards through miles of stock-brick suburbs to north, south, east, and west. At the beginning of the period, the railways were gouged out of Georgian streets and squares, and outlying suburbs and villages. Then came underground railways and an elaborate sewage system. Then more and more speculative building, more and more nondescript. Victorian London was a permanent building site. Its population soared: roughly a million in 1801; 4.5 million by 1881. In the 1840s alone, the period of the Irish famine, which killed over 1 million, 17 percent of London's population were migrants. Three hundred thirty thousand new people came to London in that decade.

Dickens, again in *Dombey and Son,* hauntingly speaks of these thousands, making their way on foot down muddy roads

and who, footsore and weary, [gazed] fearfully at the huge town before them, as if foreboding that their misery there would be but as a drop of water in the sea, or as a grain of sea-sand on the shore ... Swallowed up in one phase or other of its immensity, towards which they seemed impelled by a desperate fascination, they never returned. Food for the hospitals, the churchyards, the prisons, the river, fever, madness, vice and death—they passed on to the monster, roaring in the distance, and were lost.

The Railway Age made, and unmade, London. By the 1850s, an elaborate network of railroads connected Birmingham, the Midlands, East Anglia, Scotland, and Wales to the metropolis in a manner never dreamed of in the eighteenth century. The destruction described by Dickens affected the poor, chiefly. The railway companies could not afford to buy the properties of the rich to carve up, and a Parliamentary Royal Commission forbade the building of a railway terminus within the central area bordered by Marylebone Road, City Road, Finsbury Square, and Bishopsgate Street.

About half the navvies who built the railways were Irish. They were badly paid, and their working and living conditions were harsh: it was usual to separate families, forcing the children of navvies into dormitories while their fathers lived in lodgings with other men. The Irishmen who built the great turnstile at the bottom of Haverstock Hill, known as the Roundhouse (now a theater) staged a violent rebellion in 1846.

The riot took place in the half mile of old Hampstead Road known as Chalk Farm Road, in the hot August of 1846, at the height of the famine in Ireland. On Monday, the ninth, Railway Constable Number 145 saw a large group of Irish navvies trying to get into the building site where the English bricklayers were at work. It is impossible at this distance to know how the quarrel broke out or exactly what it was about, since when the navvies were brought before the Marylebone magistrate they were not allowed to offer any evidence or any extenuating pleas in their defense. The Irish, who had been working near the station at Primrose Hill, advanced to attack the English bricklayers. Presumably these men, whose relatives at home were starving, believed that the English had stolen their day's work? There were cries of "Kill the——— Protestant!" on the one hand, and "Murder!" by a landlady in Chalk Farm Road as she looked down on the street battle, which raged for over an hour between hundreds of laborers, hitting one another with shovels and picks. The police were beaten off and entirely failed to contain the violence. It was only when it was fizzling out that twenty Irishmen were arrested and taken to Albany Street Station. They fought so hard that it took seven constables to contain just one man.

To the authorities it was a frightening incident, not least because it demonstrated that if necessary a discontented proletariat could rise up and there would be little a police force could do against them. The Metropolitan Police had been established by Sir Robert Peel in 1829, and in this, the first major test of their strength, they had failed.

When the Chartist movement gathered momentum in

1848, the government was taking no chances. Waterloo Station was cordoned off by troops to allow the royal family to be spirited out of the capital by train and sent to their house on the Isle of Wight. Lord Fitzroy Somerset mobilized 7122 military, including cavalry; 1231 military pensioners; 4000 police; and no fewer than 85,000 special constables. The demonstration, planned for April 10, 1848, was for every man in the country to be allowed a parliamentary vote. The Whig aristocracy knew how to defend their own: they had formed a powerful alliance with the moneyed interests of the City and with the huge band of propertied Londoners, owners of small businesses, shops, and houses. The Chartists had hoped that over 100,000 would assemble on Kennington Common to march on Parliament and present their petition. As it was, about twenty thousand turned up and the occasion was a damp squib. But the government had shown its strength—with the British Museum, the Bank of England, and Somerset House all sandbagged and heavily guarded with armed men.

The contrast between Paris and London—or between London and many of the major European capitals—in this "year of revolutions" is very marked. Wretched as the plight was of the London poor, London remained an aspirant city, where those in the gutter aspired to rise. There was surprisingly little enthusiasm among the working classes in London for Chartism or any of the subsequent radical movements.

"I cares nothing for politics neither; but I'm a chartist," a street scavenger told Henry Mayhew, the journalist whose accounts of what one could almost call the ecology of London street life give us an invaluable insight into the existence of those who made a living simply out of living in London during the 1840s. In his pages we meet the blind sellers of tailor's needles, the screevers (beggars who wrote bogus letters describing their distress, which they forced into the hands of passersby) the vendors of pies, cough drops, buns, ice creams, rat poison, hare skins, live birds. From Mayhew we learn that there was hardly any old rubbish thrown out by one person that could not be sold on to another person. We meet not merely the secondhand-clothes vendors but sellers of grease, dripping, rags, and bottles.

Mayhew notes, too, the anti-Semitism of Londoners against the eighteen thousand or so Jews, mostly very poor, who live in the capital: During the eighteenth century,

> they were considered—with that exaggeration of belief dear to any ignorant community—as an entire people of misers, usurers, extortioners, receivers of stolen goods, cheats, brothel-keepers, sheriff's officers, clippers and sweaters of the coin of the realm, gaming-house keepers; in fine, the charges, or rather the accusations, of carrying on every disreputable trade, and none else, were "bundled at their doors." That there was too much foundation for many of these accusations, and still *is*, no reasonable Jew can now deny; that the wholesale prejudice against them was absurd, is equally indisputable.

Dickens's creation of Fagin falls in with this anti-Jewish stereotyping; and the modern reader is perhaps shocked by the open and unapologetic anti-Semitism of, for example, Charles Lamb, or William Makepeace Thackeray. In Mayhew, we feel it as part of the inevitable pathos and unpleasantness that result from human beings living cheek by jowl in overcrowded and often uncongenial conditions.

The overcrowding led to appalling living conditions, dreadful traffic congestion, and widespread disease. The early Victorian doctors, among them Thomas Wakley (also an MP and a coroner, who founded *The Lancet*) and John Snow (pioneer of, among other things, the use of chloroform to lessen the pains of childbirth; Queen Victoria was a patient) were in the forefront of social improvement. The governing authorities hated Wakley for making public the extent of disease. For example, though the number of deaths recorded between October and December 1847 greatly exceeded the norm, the bills of mortality—death certificates—did not mention a single case of cholera, which was the real reason for the upsurge. The cholera epidemics killed tens of thousands. In 1849, fourteen thousand Londoners died of cholera, ten thousand in 1854—yet the private water companies were still supplying Thames water for drinking to their customers. In 1866, six thousand Londoners died of the disease.

By then, Edwin Chadwick, author of the *Report on the Sanitary Conditions of the Labouring Population* (1842), had been campaigning for a quarter of a century for decent underground sewers. It was the collaboration of Snow and Chadwick that led to the creation of the London sewers, one of the engineering triumphs of the Victorians. The cast-iron pipes, sunk deep beneath the London streets, ensured that even during the heaviest bombardments of the Second World War, Londoners could count on clean drinking water. There are over four hundred miles of pipes in the main London drainage system, and some twenty-five hundred miles of subsidiary piping. The pumping system necessary to purify the sewage was not perfected until the twentieth century, but the basic infrastructure of the London sewers, which saved thousands of human lives and improved the daily existence of the living so immeasurably, was the achievement first of the social pioneers Chadwick and Snow and, of equal importance, of the engineering skills of Joseph Bazalgette.

As well as building many miles of sewers out of London stock brick, Bazalgette also constructed the vast granite Albert, Victoria, and Chelsea embankments. The visitor to the London of today must sometimes regret that it is so difficult to get to the very bank of the river which runs through its heart. This regret would not have been foremost during

Bazalgette's lifetime. Disraeli described the Thames as "a Stygian pool reeking with ineffable and unbearable horror." He did not, for once, exaggerate. The Houses of Parliament, built so picturesquely on the water's edge, sometimes had to close altogether because the stench was intolerable.

If the sewers were born of necessity, so was the other Victorian engineering miracle in London, the underground railway. The center of town was too crowded, too expensive, and too congested with horse traffic to allow the building of railways overground. Yet more and more who worked in London needed to live in its outlying suburbs, which were expanding all the time during the Victorian period. The obvious solution was to build railways underground.

The first underground railway, the steam-operated Metropolitan, was opened in March 1863. It ran four miles, from Paddington to Farringdon Street. Charles Pearson, a member of the Common Council of the City of London, was the man who came up with the brilliant idea. The extraordinary fact about him is that he began recommending it as early as the 1830s, when he saw the problems that would be created by the population growth of London. The first trains (which Londoners referred to as the Underground even before the opening in March 1863), were gaslit.

After a few disasters—subsidence, the bursting of the Fleet river near Farringdon Station during the building process, and very expensive compensation claims from those who claimed their buildings were being undermined by the railway—the "tube" was developed, based on a tunneling shield first pioneered by Marc Brunel in 1818. Isambard Brunel used such a shield for his tunnel beneath the Thames of 1843 and the first tube railway (as opposed to the "cut and cover" method by which the 1863 Metropolitan line was built) between Tower Hill and Bermondsey opened in 1870. It was cable operated. James Greathead, seeing the potential of the tube, constructed the world's first underground electric tube railway, the City and South London, in 1890.

In the construction of the sewers and the Underground, you might say that the Victorians showed themselves at their best: here is that trademark Victorian combination of public-spiritedness—a desire to improve the lot of the human race—with cleverness and engineering skill, and with the willpower to see through a brilliant notion.

Yet the Victorians' independence of mind was also manifested in their dread of government, of busybodydom, of state interference. The voluntarism by which London affairs were or were not conducted had unfortunate consequences, with some of which London is still living.

The Corporation of London, an unelected and sometimes (in those days) corrupt body, was responsible only for the Square Mile and for those other parts of the capital leased or owned by City companies or by the Corporation itself. Joshua Toulmin Smith, author of *The Metropolis and Its Municipal Administration* (1852) argued passionately that the City of London should not be forced into line under the Public Health Act. His advocacy greatly delayed Chadwick's sanitary reforms and cost many lives through cholera.

London never, for the first nine decades of the nineteenth century, had an elected body responsible for ensuring that its transport, its schools, its hospitals, its housing, its sanitation were adequate to the needs of the inhabitants. Between the ancient cities of London (the Square Mile) and Westminster, there was a chaos of boroughs and former villages. Planning, as such, was nonexistent. The architectural vandalism that resulted creates dismay in a reader of the twenty-first century.

Victorian speculative builders destroyed more Wren churches than did the Luftwaffe. *The Builder* proudly announced, "The church has to give way to commerce, vested interests in narrow streets are bought out and wide thoroughfares flanked by new structures take their place." That was in 1881.

St. Bartholomew-by-the-Exchange was demolished in 1840–41 to make way for the new Royal Exchange. St. Benet Gracechurch Street was demolished in 1867–68; the *Illustrated London News* rejoiced at the disappearance of its "ugly spire." St. Benet Fink went in the 1840s, and in 1894 were cleared out the final ruins and remains of St. Clare Minoresses without Aldgate (the other convent buildings had been destroyed by fire in 1797). St. Dionis Backchurch, where Dr. Burney had been the organist in 1749–51, was demolished in 1878. St. George Botolph Lane was pulled down as late as 1941; St. James in the Wall, 1872; St. Martin Outwich (a medieval church, which had escaped the Great Fire but had been rebuilt in 1765) was pulled down in 1874; St. Mary Somerset (one of Wren's finest) was demolished by Special Act of Parliament in 1872; St. Matthew Friday Street, a charming small church by Wren, went in 1881; St. Michael Bassishaw in 1899; St. Michael Wood Street in 1894; St. Olave Old Jewry, a Wren church of great historic interest with roots in the twelfth century, was destroyed in 1888.

It is difficult to exaggerate the Victorian hatred of the past, particularly of the eighteenth century. Think of Dickens's descriptions of Mr. Dombey's house in the elegant Portman Square: it is seen as ugly, just as Tennyson thought of the superb terraces of elegant Wimpole Street as "the long unlovely street" in *In Memoriam*. "If the Regency prized smooth stucco," wrote Donald J. Olsen in *The Growth of Victorian London*,

the Victorians produced the roughest stone surfaces possible; if the Georgians preferred unobstructive grey bricks, the Victorians produced the brightest red bricks they could manage; if the Georgians sought restrained uniform, monochrome façades, the Victorians revelled in glazed, polychrome tiles; if the Georgians admired flat cornices topping their buildings, the Victorians sought jagged skylines; if the Georgians desired uniformity, the Victorians demanded variety.

The architectural monuments which they have left to us tell us much about the Victorian multiple personality, now building a Gothic railway station such as St. Pancras, now blocks of flats or shops in a "Queen Anne" manner.

With the ease of travel brought about by the railways, there was a growth of hotels; Philip Hardwick's Great Western Royal Hotel at Paddington Station (1854) was an inseparable part of traveling westwards by rail. Until very recently, you could walk directly from the hotel onto the station platform. This was the era not only of the great station hotels but also of hotels within the metropolis itself. Hitherto, only aristocrats or their imitators would have taken whole houses for a "season," bringing with them from the country their servants and retinue. Now, anyone prepared to pay could come up and stay in London without "knowing anyone." The Westminster Palace Hotel in Victoria Street opened in 1860 with three hundred bedrooms, fourteen bathrooms, and the first lifts in London. By the end of the century Richard D'Oyly Carte, flush with the success of Gilbert and Sullivan's operas, which he had managed and produced, built the legendary Savoy Hotel, with electric lights, lifts, and every luxury. In 1899, Cesar Ritz had opened the Carlton Hotel in the Haymarket, and the hotel that bore his name opened in 1906.

The hotel was a deeply Victorian institution. The hotel is the natural refuge of the family on the move, of the commercial traveler, of the surreptitious liaison and the hidden life. As Oscar Wilde says, in John Betjeman's poem, before his arrest at the Cadogan Hotel in Chelsea—

One astrakhan coat is at Willis's
Another one's at the Savoy;
So fetch my morocco portmanteau
And bring them on later, dear boy....

The Victorians made much of the cult of home and for that reason needed refuges from it. The simple chophouses and coffeehouses of a previous age survived. But restaurants became popular, ranging from the very grand, such as the Café Royal in Regent Street (opened in 1865) to the more bohemian, such as Kettner's in Soho. (Both, at the time of writing, are still extant.)

Some of the restaurants, such as Spiers or Pond's Criterion at Piccadilly Circus, were huge. It was now possible for women to eat out, alone, or accompanied by other women, or with their husbands. As well as theaters, there was another attraction luring the inhabitants of the suburbs into the centers: department stores. These expanded and grew during the 1880s and 1890s, from William Whiteley's (founded 1863), the Civil Service Stores (1865), and the Army and Navy Stores (1871). Smallish drapers, such as Swan and Edgar (1812), Dickins and Jones (1837) (they started as Dickins and Smith in 1790), and Marshall and Snelgrove (1837) grew to match their rivals. Harrods, a small grocery shop that had originated in the East End, moved to Knightsbridge and became an institution, providing services such as a lending library, a bank, and an undertaker's. As the artist Osbert Lancaster observed, "All my female relatives had their own favourites, where some of them had been honoured customers for more than half a century, and their arrival was greeted by frenzied bowing on the part of the frock-coated shopwalkers.... For my Great-aunt Bessie the Army and Navy Stores fulfilled all the functions of her husband's club" (*All Done from Memory,* p. 35).

The men's clubs flourished as never before. Social climbing was such a universal form of exercise in the late nineteenth century that there could not be enough establishments priding themselves on being exclusively for gentlemen. Just as the public schools with pretensions to grandeur, such as Eton and Harrow, spawned hundreds of imitators for those lower down the social scale, so White's and Brooks's had a host of imitators, some for army officers, some for civil servants, some for the self-consciously raffish or bohemian. They were all ways of defining the persona of those who applied for membership, and they were all ways of escaping home.

Home need no longer be a house in the ever growing suburbs. Just as work could now be in a purpose-built office block (erected in all likelihood on the site of some lovely Georgian terrace or Wren church), home could be in a flat. Francophobia made the English slow to copy the Parisian zest for flat life, but its economic practicality and its offer of privacy were both tempting. In the mid-1850s, three-quarters of Londoners were huddled together cheek by jowl in lodging houses of one description or another. By the end, this number had been much reduced and Londoners were beginning the standoffish existence which is now their norm, with their own multiplicity of dwellings with their own front doors.

By the end of the century, blocks of mansion flats dominated Victoria Street, Chelsea Embankment, Cadogan Square, Kensington High Street, and much of Bloomsbury. These substantial and secluded residences are no hermitages. They all have rooms for servants. More than a fifth of Londoners were in domestic service, and servant's quarters were an obvious way of housing the poor. If you had to choose between a maid's bedroom in Pont Street, Knightsbridge, and a shared room in some squalid lodging house in Wapping or Hackney, it is not hard to know which option would be more comfortable.

London's failure to address the problems of the poor, and in particular their need for accommodation, was a Victorian scandal, which generations of philanthropy did very little to change. Cheap housing supplied by individual philanthropists such as the Baroness Burdett-Coutts, or the Peabody Trust (founded by the American George Peabody, who had been impressed by Lord Shaftesbury's work for the dispossessed) simply could not keep up with the demand and the numbers of people who needed to be housed.

No wonder the poor took refuge when they could in the pub, and no wonder so much of the humor of the music halls, which began life in pubs, is about drunkenness, dispossession, and the sexual humiliations to be found in such circumstances. Marie Lloyd, one of the greatest performers on the English stage, was born Matilda Alice Victoria Wood at 36 Plumber Street, in the slums of Hoxton. She died in 1922. Her cynical, boozy songs were about the world which she and her audiences were forced by economic circumstances to inhabit.

Only in 1889 did London finally have a properly elected local authority of its own, to match the civic authorities that had transformed Birmingham, Bradford, and Leeds into places that had begun to solve some of their worst social problems. In the 1870s in Birmingham, the radical mayor, Joseph Chamberlain, had the power to raise rates, municipalize the utilities, and take out loans for schemes of public works. No such body existed in London until the London County Council, the LCC, was set up.

From the first, the central government viewed the LCC with the deepest suspicion. The Liberals (or Progressives, as they called themselves in the elections) won control of the first LCC over the Moderates (or Conservatives) in January 1889. Conservative central government did its best, under the cynical Lord Salisbury, to make the LCC unworkable by creating twenty-eight metropolitan boroughs whose vestries and boards would have autonomy. Gas, water, and electricity were not in the hands of the LCC, nor initially was any overall authority for sanitation, street cleaning, refuse collection, or local drains. Nevertheless, a start had been made. The LCC presided over 117 square miles; it was composed of 126 councillors elected every three years, and twenty-one aldermen elected by those councillors for periods of six years. It was the first time since the Roman Londinium that there had been one single controlling authority attempting to administer the chaos that called itself London.

As the national capital, London was the obvious place to provide shows and demonstrations of patriotic achievement. In 1851, in the middle of Hyde Park, in Paxton's great Crystal Palace, the preeminence of British industry was presented to the world in the Great Exhibition. It attracted huge crowds and made so much money that on the strength of it they could build the Albertopolis, the assembly of buildings in South Kensington that includes the Victoria and Albert Museum and the Royal Albert Hall, as well as the Natural History and Science Museums.

At the end of the century, in 1887 and 1897, London staged the Golden and Diamond Jubilees of the Queen, with royal pageantry and military parades, and services in St. Paul's Cathedral. Yet, when she went to the East End, Queen Victoria was booed. The event that dominated the close of her reign in London was not the Jubilee but the dock strike, when thirty thousand men bravely forwent pay, and risked the hunger of their families, by striking and showing the world that they could not subsist on the wages offered. They were campaigning for a princely sixpence an hour.

Now, as we survey what is left of Victorian London, we can be sentimental about its architectural remains. The stained or decorated glass and varnished mahogany and pine of the old pubs; the incense-drowned mystery of brick churches; the cavernous cathedral grandeur of St. Pancras Station can take us back to a dream Victorian London, where Sherlock Holmes rides in a hansom cab through the fog and housemaids behind shuttered bedroom windows allow their lecherous employers to unribbon their stays. No doubt such jollities could be found. No doubt we would have enjoyed a club dinner with Trollope or gone out whistling into the night had we attended the first night of the *Mikado* at the Savoy Theatre. But we should have done so knowing that in arches under the embankment barefoot children starved to death. In the capital of the richest empire the world had ever seen was poverty that would compare with the most deprived parts of Africa or South America in the twenty-first century.

10

1900–1939

In 1932 the Lordship Lane Recreation Ground was opened in the northern suburb of Tottenham, a working-class area to the south of the White Hart Estate. Half this land was given over to allotments, little strips of ground where people could grow their own flowers and vegetables, build wooden huts for their garden tools or for amorous adventures, and indulge the sense that, though their living accommodation was restricted, they possessed a garden. The sky was above their heads and the earth beneath their feet. This sensation was—is—especially precious to those who dwell in flats or tenements.

Herbert Morrison (1888–1965) became the leader of the London County Council in 1934, but he had been intimately involved with London politics since early manhood, becoming secretary of the London Labour Party when he was twenty-seven, in April 1915. He was the youngest of seven children of an alcoholic policeman from Brixton and Priscilla Lyon, the daughter of an East End carpet fitter. He was blind in one eye, after an easily treatable eye infection during boyhood received no treatment. (School friends called him Ball of Fat because of the dead appearance of the sightless eye.)

Morrison dominated the Labour Party on a national level and was to become Deputy Prime Minister to Attlee in the government of 1945. He came to his moderate Socialist beliefs neither from the trade union movement, of which he formed no part, nor from the middle-class, university-fed intelligentsia. He was circulation manager on the *Daily Citizen* and his political education was formed, like that of many

Londoners, by reading newspapers and attending political meetings and street-corner speeches. It was hearing such legendary figures as Keir Hardie and George Bernard Shaw speaking that had led to his joining the Independent Labour Party in 1906. He was elected to Parliament as a London MP and he represented Hackney South from 1923 to 1929, having been mayor of Hackney since 1919. As a minister in Ramsay MacDonald's Labour government he had responsibility for transport, and brought in the Road Traffic Act of 1930 and the London Transport Act of 1933. When MacDonald horrified his Socialist colleagues by forming a national government in 1933, Morrison, initially tempted to stay in power, resigned and lost his parliamentary seat; as a result, he could concentrate his energies on London politics and the LCC.

The Lordship Lane Recreation Ground is a good place to stand and think about the career of Morrison and his brand of London Socialism. One of Morrison's dreams, as leader of the LCC, was to establish a green belt around London, a lung for an overcrowded city. A reflection of Morrison's interest in a publicly coordinated transport system is also reflected in Lordship Lane, for here was constructed, for the children of the White Hart Lane Estate, a fantasy of Socialist order. Around the boating lake and the bandstand and the tennis courts, the superintendent of parks, Mr. G. E. Paris, F. Inst.PA FRHS created a plan of a "model traffic area" laid out like a model village but with real roads, fully operative traffic lights, and pedal cars that could be hired for a halfpenny per half hour. Traffic jams could be engineered by real miniature traffic signs: "Halt at Major Road Ahead." There was tremendous excitement on the opening day, with local newspapers recording that five hundred children queued from eight A.M. for tickets.

Today, inevitably, the model traffic area barely survives. The road network has been vandalized. Some crudely relandscaped hillocks with sliced-up motor tires cater for an already dead craze for mountain biking. Anyone with the temerity to walk in the park today is more likely to encounter a sex maniac released into the community, or a heroin addict shooting up, than the ghost of the ex–taxi driver who, in a peaked cap, directed the traffic in 1938 and controlled the working Belisha beacons, the pedestrian cross ng lights.[1]

Morrison had stood for election to the leadership of the London County Council (LCC) on a program of optimistic Socialism: "Up with the Houses! Down with the Slums!" In its first three-year term, the Labour-dominated LCC displaced and rehoused 34,036 people, very many more than had been rehoused by previous councils. In 1936–39 it built an average of four thousand flats annually, four times more than had been built annually between 1930 and 1934. Between 1934 and 1939 nearly twenty thousand families from inner East London—Shoreditch, Stepney, Bethnal Green, Poplar, Bermondsey, Southwark—were rehoused, but only 4,500 new LCC dwellings were built in those neighborhoods. The tendency was to move families outwards in the vast sprawl of council flats and ribbon roads that characterized the London of the interwar years. It was not merely the working classes who moved outwards. The transport development that exemplified the social change was the building of two new electric lines by the Metropolitan Railway—to Watford, Amersham, and Uxbridge in 1925; to Stanmore in 1932.

> Hearts are light, eyes are brighter,
> In Metroland, Metroland

went the lyric by George R. Simms. "Stake your claim in Edgware," instructed an Underground booklet:

Omar Khayyám's recipe for turning the wilderness into Paradise hardly fits an English climate, but provision has been made at Edgware of an alternative recipe which at least will convert pleasant, undulating fields into happy homes. The loaf of bread, the jug of wine and the book of verse may be got there cheaply and easily, and apart from what is said by the illustration, a shelter which comprises all the latest labour-saving and sanitary conveniences. We moderns ask much more before we are content than the ancients, and Edgware is designed to give us that much more.

There are many moving things about this advertisement, not least the level of education which it expects from first-time home buyers. The British had, since the beginning of the eighteenth century, considered that a problem exported is a problem solved. In the nineteenth century, criminals and indigent Celts were exported or transported to Canada, New Zealand, and Australia, and this was one vital ingredient in the fact that there was no English revolution in 1848, no Commune in London as there was in Paris in 1870.

———

Every London fire station, railway station, post office mail-sorting center, gentlemen's club, council office, and town hall has its war memorial, testifying to the devastation of losses at the front. But chiefly the First World War was, for Londoners, a nightmare happening elsewhere. It is true that there were bombing raids. The first was on May 31, 1915, when a German airship dropped a ton of bombs. But during the whole of the First World War, the total of Londoners killed by air raids was 670, a dreadful number if you happened to be their friend, husband, parent, but not to be compared with the many thousands of civilians across Europe who were destined to be killed by aerial bombardment during the Second World War.

Those who came back from the fighting had been promised a land fit for heroes to live in. They found that some things had changed forever, most notably in the lives of women. It was an American, Lady Astor, who in 1919 became the first woman MP. She had played no part in the feminist movement. Emmeline Pankhurst, the greatest campaigner for women's suffrage, failed to win a seat in the election that took Nancy Astor to the House of Commons. She agreed to contest Whitechapel (as a Conservative) in 1926, but died before the election.

The implosion of the Independent Labour Party, the betrayal (as the Socialists saw it) of their cause by Ramsay MacDonald after 1931, happened against a background of economic and political turmoil. After the Wall Street crash of 1929, it seemed perfectly plausible that the prophecies of Karl Marx were about to be fulfilled and that capitalism itself was collapsing. All over the United States and Europe, dreadful hardship was suffered as unemployment soared.

The Independent Labour Party had never been wholly Marxist in outlook, but it shared the underlying Marxist supposition that capital oppressed rather than enriched the working man. It might have been supposed that the Labour government of Ramsay MacDonald, or his Chancellor of the Exchequer, Philip Snowden, would have rejoiced at the consummation of their hopes. With capital in ruins, it was surely now time for the state to intervene, with schemes of public works, unemployment benefits, and housing benefits, to soften the blow of the crisis and to pave the way for a new era in which private enterprise and selfishness were banished and subsumed in a common cause in which all pulled together.

Instead, MacDonald and Snowden, who had learnt their Socialism from the great nineteenth-century legends—Keir Hardie, William Morris, and the rest—pursued no such policy. From 1924, when he became Chancellor, Snowden had in fact abandoned Socialism and had cut taxes. His commitment to free trade and the market "righting itself" was positively

Gladstonian. While MacDonald and Snowden, at the behest of the King, abandoned Socialism and the Socialists, unemployment soared.

It is not surprising that there should have been dismay. During a speech in Trafalgar Square on September 14, 1931, Ramsay MacDonald's young chancellor of the Duchy of Lancaster, who had resigned in protest at the government's failure to address the appalling unemployment crisis, said:

> Spokesmen of the late Labour Government saw in the crisis that collapse of capitalism which they had prophesied with religious fervour. The crisis came in a lucky moment for them. Labour was in office, and had every resource of the State at its command. What happened? The great day dawned, and Labour resigned; cleared out just when they had the realization of their greatest wish. What must we think of a Salvation Army which takes to its heels on the Day of Judgement?

The speaker was Sir Oswald Mosley, a baronet, a First World War hero, and a Staffordshire squire, who had been by turns a Tory and a Socialist MP. During the year of his break with Labour, 1931, and his formation of something called the New Party, unemployment had risen to 2,642,000. The following year it was to rise to 2,756,000; thereafter it sank, gradually, to 1,408,000 in 1939.

The humiliations and deprivations which these figures represent in millions of British families can barely be guessed in today's comfortable world. This was the era of the hated means test, when dole money was refused if a household possessed so much as a silver teapot, and inspectors called at working-class households to rummage through people's belongings. The Jarrow Hunger March in 1936, in which the destitute workers of the northeast walked to the capital, has never been forgotten. In the provinces, where people tended to rely upon one or two local industries for work, there was little or no chance for them to get "on their bike" to find alternative employment. If the local mines or mills or shipyard were laying men off, the workers were sunk, their families condemned to near starvation. Dame Janet Vaughan, who worked as a doctor in the poorer parts of London during this era, once described to me conditions in the tenements—malnourished children with rickets who had no shoes; diseases that as an educated young doctor she had supposed had gone out of existence in the nineteenth century. "You could *only* be a Socialist in such circumstances," she said simply.

Because of the dire situation in the provinces, many came to the capital to find work; the population of Greater London between 1911 and 1939 swelled from 7.25 to 8.73 million.

"You could only be a Socialist," but Morrison's chirpy election promise—"Up with the Houses! Down with the Slums!"—was only partially working. Two factors led Londoners, in very substantial numbers, to flock to Sir Oswald Mosley's call, first to his New Party and then to his British Union of Fascists.

The first was a dread of Communism, which had plunged Russia into a bloody civil war, followed by the worst tyranny ever known in the history of the human race. In Germany, Austria, Hungary, France, and other European countries, the economic crisis had led to anarchy, greatly exacerbated, as many believed, by Communist agitators, who positively wanted the system to collapse.

The second and more important factor in Mosley's popularity was the singular failure of the Labour Party to address the desperate plight of the unemployed. Those out of work, and those who dreaded losing their work, believed him correct in his advocacy of the economics of John Maynard Keynes, his belief that a government could borrow its way out of the unemployment crisis and create an artificial labor market. Combined with this Keynesian sleight of hand, Mosley had an extraordinary eloquence. "It was better than a visit to the theater," one old Londoner once said to me, fondly recalling Sir Oswald's speeches. The Labour movement had looked to him: "How wide across all parties was the fascination which Mosley exercised," Michael Foot once wrote; and the ex-Communist firebrand Mannie Shinwell wrote in 1952 that "almost everyone expected that, because of his popularity, [Mosley] would replace Ramsay Macdonald."

The photographs speak for themselves—whole streets in Limehouse, or Bermondsey, packed with working men giving Mosley the Fascist salute; Trafalgar Square, and even Hyde Park, in 1934, packed. The last of his huge rallies, in July 1939 in the Earl's Court Exhibition Hall, was reported to be the largest indoor meeting ever to take place, anywhere in the world.

Yet, although in his book *My Life* Mosley talks of "our electoral triumph," this in fact refers to a few seats on borough councils and, in general elections, a polling of 19 percent of the electorate in one sympathetic constituency. Mosley's Fascist party never won a single parliamentary seat and this charismatic figure, deemed only a few years before so popular that he would inevitably become leader of the Labour Party and then prime minister, did not even win a seat himself.

The truth is that although the Fascist rallies were impressive, they did not offer any real hope of a solution to the unemployment crisis. Mosley admitted in retrospect that it had been a mistake to adopt uniforms, making his movement seem like an imitation of Mussolini's in Italy. With the rise of Hitler in Germany, the behavior of a minority of Blackshirt thugs in London's East End made the movement repellent to the ordinary decent voter. Mosley showed no sign of being personally anti-Semitic, but he was willing to subscribe to conspiracy theories about international Jewry to bring about the result he wanted, a war. It was hard to see how his mission in the cause of the British working man was helped by associating with bullies who marched through poorer districts in the East End, chanting "The yids, the yids, we've got to get rid of the yids," or smashing the windows of synagogues or small shopkeepers and tailors. Such behavior was intolerable and the violence at Mosley's rallies (largely started, he always maintained, by left-wing agitators) led to a parliamentary ban on his bizarre uniforms, which resembled those of a strutting fencing master in some Ruritanian mountain kingdom.

The rallies of the British Union of Fascists, when seen in the context of the history of London, seem less like imitations of Mussolini or foreshadowings of the Third Reich than like 1930s versions of the age-old ability of Londoners to take to the streets and then retreat home, without any obvious change having taken place. They rallied for Wilkes and Liberty, but they did not rampage, as the French would have done, until they got them. They spent a few days setting fire to jails and embassy chapels, shouting themselves hoarse against Popery for Lord George Gordon. But after three days, the Pope seemed no more of a threat than the Shah of Persia. They flocked to Kennington Common in the rain to support the Charter, and then waited seventy patient years before the vote was offered to every adult in the land.

George Orwell, in *The Road to Wigan Pier,* said that "fish and chips, art-silk stockings, tinned salmon, cut-price chocolates, the movies, the radio, strong tea and the Football Pools have between them averted revolution." Would be revolutionaries have often been shocked (as Lenin was when he spent a year living in London) by the English capacity to switch off politically. This capacity, less marked in the Irish, Welsh, and Scots, has been a repeated pattern of London political existence. In the diary he kept before writing *Wigan Pier,* Orwell noted, "There is no *turbulence* left in England."

———

In a period which was by and large undistinguished architecturally in London, a few buildings and architects stand out as being of outstanding and enduring merit. No one who drives into London by the A40 can fail to be uplifted by the proportions, color, and beauty of the Hoover factory near Perivale, built to designs by Wallis Gilbert and Partners in 1932–33. The BBC used good architects for their two great broadcasting centers in London. Bush House, home to the World Service of the BBC, is by the American architects Helmle and Corbett, completed in 1935. Nikolaus Pevsner, the great architectural historian, tells us, "It represents a big-business classicism which the Americans handled more successfully than the English, and Bush House has without doubt more distinction than the other Kingsway buildings."

Broadcasting House itself in Portland Place is by the Arts and Crafts architect Charles Holden (1875–1960). With its Eric Gill relief of Ariel, this noble building is not only a thing of great beauty but also a symbol of all that the British Broadcasting Corporation once was, central to London and civilization, a beacon of truth telling and decency, now threatened by its own suited executives, who mistake it for a commercial station like any other. (Under the director-generalship of Sir John Birt, they even wanted to leave this great building, with all its associations; and it has been painfully wrecked inside.) Charles Holden was the best architect of the interwar years in London. His Senate House in the University of London Bloomsbury, is another truly great building, and it is to Holden that we owe so many excellent Underground stations, of which Arnos Grove is the classic expression.

More overt attempts at modernism such as Lubetkin and Tecton's Highpoint blocks of flats on North Hill, Highgate (built between 1935 and 1938), have the air of having been insolently set down regardless of their setting. Their Penguin Pool at London Zoo (1934), being of smaller scale, continues to amuse but only as a joke. If you measure a penguin against Lubetkin's strange geometrical walkways, and a human being against one of his blocks of flats, you begin to have a frisson of dismay, a foretaste of what crudely modernist architecture was going to do to London in the years to come.

Some of the jollier buildings of the period, though hardly great works of architecture, were the cinemas—Frank Verity's Odeon (formerly the Pavilion) at Shepherd's Bush (1923), or the Regal by E. Norman Bailey in Uxbridge High Street. Older cinema style can be appreciated, incidentally, in the wonderful refurbishment by Simon Wedgwood and Faithful Blyth of the Electric Cinema in Notting Hill, dating from 1911, with its detailed classical façade, its fluted pilasters in faience and its barrel-vaulted auditorium.

It was in cinemas that Londoners, in the first four decades of the twentieth century, both escaped and confronted the gathering storm, since as well as the hypnotic escape of westerns, farces, romances, these same screens were those on which the audiences, nearly all smoking cigarettes, watched the unfolding dramatic tragedy of the 1930s: a Berlin Olympic Games staged like a National Socialist propaganda rally; the occupation by German troops of the Sudetenland; the Italian bombardment of Ethiopia; the Spanish Civil War. Crumbling buildings, gunfire, crowds roaring their enthusiasm in huge stadia for sporting heroes or gesticulating dictators, rolling tanks and the British Prime Minister at an airport, waving a piece of paper on which he had collected Herr Hitler's guarantee of "Peace in our time"—these shared the bill with Charlie Chaplin and the cartoon character dismissed by the King Emperor George V as "that damned mouse." Karl Marx was momentarily forgotten as they laughed at his namesakes

Groucho, Harpo, Chico, and Zeppo in *Monkey Business, Horse Feathers,* and *Duck Soup.* Here, too, they could see the films which the great Hungarian director Alexander Korda produced with London Film Productions at Denham Studios, starting with *The Private Life of Henry VIII* in 1932 or shriek with laughter at Will Hay in *Boys Will Be Boys* or *Oh, Mr. Porter!.*

———

By the end of the 1930s the world elsewhere, the European catastrophe, was coming to London, not just on the flickering screens of the cinemas, but in a huge increase in the refugee population. Whereas at most ten thousand refugees from Germany had arrived between 1933 and 1938, events now changed all that. Following the union of Austria and Germany (*Anschluss*) and the Crystal Night, when Jewish businesses, synagogues, schools, and houses were smashed or attacked by arsonists, the number of Jews arriving in Britain grew dramatically.

Tragic as were its causes, the arrival of so many refugees from the mainstream of cultural and intellectual life in Europe had the most invigorating effect on London. The strange outcome of the huge increase in London's population up to 1939 had been to make it more, not less, homogeneous since, until the refugees from Hitler leavened the lump, nearly all the newcomers to London were English provincials and almost all of them chose to remain in the suburbs. London had never been bigger, but it had never seemed less cosmopolitan than when the majority of its inhabitants commuted to and fro on bus or electric train between offices in inner London and small houses in Surrey or Middlesex. At last, for the first time since the immigrations of the nineteenth century, London reverted to its norm, with different languages being spoken in its streets and sizable numbers in search of food which was not available at the Lyons Cornerhouse café or the plain English grocer. The refugees enabled London once again to be itself, the city of Huguenot weavers, lascar sailors, Dutch merchants, and liberated African or Caribbean slaves.

In the eighteen months between March 1938 and September 1939, sixty thousand were admitted from Germany. Of Vienna's 180,000 Jews, thirty thousand came to Britain as their first port of call. The rescue of Jewish children, the scheme known as the *Kindertransport,* brought ten thousand children to Britain, perhaps a tenth of all the Jewish children left in the Reich.

Although the Jews were being persecuted in the countries now dominated by the Reich, deprived of professional status, their assets confiscated, their right to study at university curtailed or removed, their movement restricted, comparatively few had actually been killed. Their outright massacre was, according to Hitler in *Mein Kampf,* part of his endgame, but few could really believe that he intended—or was in a position—to carry out a scheme so monstrous or so absolutely deadly. With hindsight, many of the British Foreign Office and Home Office personnel who quibbled about visas and entry permits for German Jews must have wished that all six million had been invited to Britain.

The consequence in the immediate to mid-term of the tragedy was, as far as London was concerned, an unmixed blessing. Sigmund Freud arrived in Primrose Hill (later to move to Maresfield Gardens) with his celebrated couch and his collection of fetishistic sculptures. Karl Rankl, Fritz Busch, Alexander Korda, Elias Canetti, Friedrich von Hayek, Nikolaus Pevsner, Ernst Gombrich ... It would be possible to fill page after page with the names of those who have enormously enriched the musical, artistic, academic, scientific, philosophical life of London because of Hitler's maniac anti-Semitism.

None of these people were given state handouts or dole money just for being "asylum seekers." Educated and middle-class Jews took any work that was offered to them. In the "Situations Wanted" columns of the papers it was commonplace to read such ads as "Will any kindhearted people help bring husband out of Vienna? Wife already here; first-class cook and dressmaker; desire post together anywhere."

Others, more fortunate, fled Hitler's lands with jewels or gold sewn into their clothing and would turn up in Belsize Park offering to buy flats or even houses with their portable capital. The huge majority were not so fortunate and a large number had to endure years of poverty before getting themselves established. Many felt themselves to be exploited by their English (Jewish or Gentile) employers, who tried to turn a blind eye to the emotional trauma they were undergoing, separated from their endangered loved ones at home in Austria or Germany.[2]

In all the tension and buildup to war during the first nine months of 1939, and in all the feelings of guilt and hope following the Munich agreement, national fears focused on the destiny of London. A week before war broke out, Vita Sackville-West wrote to her husband, Harold Nicolson, "If only you were not in London. It makes me physically sick to think of air-raids."[3]

As Londoners watched the international fiasco happen, they hoped against hope for peace and prepared for war. Sir John Anderson, chairman of the Committee of Imperial Defence, believed that London would be the immediate target of aerial bombardment. His committee calculated that two thousand tons would be dropped by the Germans in the first twenty-four hours. They calculated a death roll of 28,000 civilians in the first month. In *Which Way to Peace?*, the philosopher Bertrand Russell predicted that London would be "one vast raving bedlam, the hospitals will be stormed, traffic will cease, the homeless will shriek for peace, the city will be pandemonium."[4]

At eleven A.M. on September 3, Neville Chamberlain told anxious wireless listeners that Britain was at war with Germany. An hour passed; twenty-four hours; and still no bombs, no destruction. Apart from the sandbags piled up against windows and in doorways, and apart from a palpable atmosphere of tension and excitement, London seemed much as normal. But it was about to enter into the six most extraordinary years of its history. The bombs would come, though not at once. Some traffic would be stopped. Some would shriek for peace. But a much stranger thing was going to happen than Bertrand Russell's vision of pandemonium.

11

WARTIME
1939–1945

The photograph, by Herbert Mason, of St. Paul's Cathedral on December 29–30, 1940, expresses an unalterable historical truth and a tragically false prophecy. They called it the Second Great Fire of London. Since September, London had been the chief, almost the exclusive, target of a relentless series of raids by German bombers: 27,500 high-explosive bombs and innumerable incendiaries were dropped, on average 160 bombers attacking nightly, between September 7 and November 13. The docks were a prime target, often in flames, the dwellings of the poor who lived nearby were reduced to street after street of smoking rubble. Buildings as familiar as Madame Tussaud's in Baker Street and the Tower of London had been hit by bombs. The Guildhall was all but gutted by fire on that clear moonlit night of December 29, 1940. And it was after that air raid that Herbert Mason's camera captured St. Paul's, its dome clearly visible in all the smoke and flames, an orderly embodiment of calm and reason, of the English enlightenment, of piety, and of the past in all the tempests of war.

The photograph is testimony to a truth: namely that London endured regular bombardment with extraordinary sangfroid. The courage of Londoners set a wonderful example to other cities when their turn came. St. Paul's in the flames, but unburnt like the mystic bush of Moses, told the world that though everyone else in Europe had surrendered to Nazism, or formed unworthy alliances with it, the capital city of the British empire would do no such thing.

So much for the historical truth. The photograph also, by implication, speaks a prophecy that

> This England never did, nor never shall,
> Lie at the proud foot of a conqueror.[1]

The photograph seems to say, "When this war is over, the London that Christopher Wren created will return: the London where reason and learning go hand in hand with commerce and trade, and where the citizens make homes, theatres, churches, and streets for themselves that are objects of beauty." This prophecy, or defiant hope, was never realized. The victors who rose from the ruins of wartime London were vandals, property speculators, modernist fanatics, and shysters. The very ownership of the City, its firms, its institutions, and its buildings, would pass out of British hands and London would be sold so that a few semicriminals could make a quick buck. No one, however, could have guessed this during the amazing six years when London was at war.

The French philosopher Simone Weil, who had spent the earlier part of the war with her parents in New York, had returned to Europe and worked for the Free French. She yearned for martyrdom and, denied the chance to return to France, she wasted away, tubercular, chain-smoking, anorexic, dying at a sanatorium at Ashford, Kent, in August 1943, aged thirty-four. She was only one of millions in London during the war, but there is an aptness about this stubborn and completely sui generis figure of genius gravitating towards the unconquerable London. She lodged in Notting Hill at 31 Portland Road (not, in those days, the fashionable street it has since become), with a schoolteacher's widow, a Mrs. Francis, who had two children. She went everywhere on foot, noting the "utterly special atmosphere of the pubs in the working-class districts. I tenderly love this city with its wounds. What strikes me most about these people, in their present situation, is a good humour that is neither spontaneous nor artificial but that comes from a feeling of fraternal and tender comradeship in a common ordeal."[2]

The sufferings inflicted upon civilian populations by aerial bombardment were one of the grisly novelties of the Second World War. When placed alongside the casualties inflicted by Allied bombardment on Hamburg and Berlin, or by the Americans on Hiroshima and Nagasaki, the actual figures of those slain by German bombs in London were, by the horrific standards of that conflict, comparatively small. Tens of thousands died. Of 147,000 serious or fatal casualties caused by bombardment in Britain, 80,000 were in London (29,890 killed and 50,000 badly injured), and 1.5 million homes were destroyed. But London was still recognizable at the end of it, scarred, ruinous, but recognizable. By the end of the Battle of Berlin in 1945, 70 percent of the city would have been completely flattened. Sir Arthur Harris of Bomber Command had ordered an astounding 14,562 sorties over the German capital. As well as killing tens of thousands of Germans, these raids killed many Russian prisoners of war, working in Berlin as slaves and denied the refuge of the air-raid shelters.

It has been said that bombing cities forces the inhabitants, almost against their will, into a spirit of bravery and defiance. Yet Alexandra Richie, whose thousand-page *Faust's Metropolis* must be the best history of a city written in modern times, states, "Despite...preparations Berliners never developed the spirit which characterized London during the Blitz, not least because of the increasing presence of the Gestapo, and the bossy air-raid wardens, who bullied people with endless new regulations."[3]

In perhaps the most brilliant piece of fiction to come out of wartime London, *The Heat of the Day* by Elizabeth Bowen, it is noted that "In that September [1940] transparency people became transparent, only to be located by the just darker flicker of their hearts. Strangers saying "Good night, good luck" to each other at street corners, as the sky first balanced then faded with evening, each hoped not to die that night, still more not to die unknown."[4]

The number of Londoners evacuated from the capital was 700,000—mostly the poor, mostly children. It would seem as if the overall exodus from the capital by the outbreak of war was 1.2 million, or 13 percent of the population. By Christmas 1939, half the evacuees who had left the capital had returned. It is difficult to be certain of figures. Some evacuees settled down to their very different lives, being billeted on families in the country. The poorest of them, verminous, undisciplined, and ill clad, unacquainted with such niceties as lavatory paper or soap, and psychologically disturbed into bed-wetting, were not always welcome to their more genteel hosts.[5]

For the Londoners themselves, the tedium of country life palled. ("They call this spring, Mum, and they have one down here every year.") Many homesick families would prefer to be united in a half-ruined house in London than to be separated from their loved ones. When their homes were bombed they were herded into inadequate refuges, often set up by the local vicar, in church halls, schools, and the like. Those lucky enough had Anderson shelters or Morrison shelters built in their gardens. Far more went down into the Underground stations. By late September 1940, 177,000 people were sleeping in the Underground system. It was more than a shelter against bombs. It was a place where, quite literally, Londoners clung together, a return to the shared beds of childhood or even to the mysterious darkness of the womb itself. In Henry Moore's unforgettable drawings of these figures curled in their makeshift bedding all, even the old, have something of the air of sleeping children.

The atmosphere in London was tense, but there was great

pride about carrying on in defiance of the bombs. "Business as usual" was the motto. The great thing was not to fuss, but there was also not merely intensity but intense excitement. Sexual feeling was high. In the absolute darkness of the blackout, Anything Went. Strangers made love. The historian A. L. Rowse had his only sexual experience in ninety years of life during the blackout, coming home to his club and bumping into a man who said he was a policeman.[6] The knowledge that you might be killed any night was balanced with the heady knowledge next morning that you were still alive. A young woman whose house had been bombed wrote,

> I've been bombed.... I lay there feeling indescribably happy and triumphant. "I've been bombed!" I kept on saying to myself, over and over again—trying the phrase on, like a new dress to see how it fitted.... It seems a terrible thing to say, when many people were killed and injured last night; but never in my whole life have I ever experienced such *pure and flawless happiness.*

At the center of this extraordinary and overcharged atmosphere sat the Prime Minister, a figure who throughout his political career had always seemed too colorful, too interesting, too bombastic to fit into the dull grays of the political spectrum and whose career stretched from the Dardanelles to the Siege of Sidney Street to a long period of exile making speeches denouncing Gandhi from the back benches of the House of Commons and writing articles for the *Daily Mail* defending Edward VIII or the British empire. Then had come his moment, and Britain's.

"War's a brain-spattering, windpipe-slitting art," as Byron reminds us,[7] and when the prissy, dithering figure of Neville Chamberlain took to his sickbed, Britain took Churchill to their hearts. To visit the cabinet War Rooms beneath King

Charles Street is to be reminded, as no book can remind us, of the extraordinary atmosphere of those times and the extraordinary quality of the man who directed operations down there. He did not often sleep there, and he had small regard for his personal safety, enjoying sitting on the roof at George Street to get a better view of the air raids. But he was sometimes obliged to sleep underground; and there may still be seen his modest bedroom and the range of weaponry, including a Tommy gun, with which he proposed to defend himself had invasion occurred and his bunker been penetrated by Nazis.

His daily routine became legendary and exhausted all who worked with him—cabinet ministers, chiefs of staff, long-suffering secretaries. He woke about 8:30 A.M., lit a cigar with his bedside candle, and, wearing his green and gold silk dressing gown decorated with dragon motifs, he would hold court, read all the newspapers, dictate letters, and plan the day. By mid-morning, he was ready to soak in the bathtub while holding military discussions with General Alan Brooke (later Field Marshal Lord Alanbrooke) or General Sir Hastings Ismay, who in 1944 threatened resignation because of Churchill's irascibility. Lunch and dinner were always accompanied by champagne. He had an afternoon nap, but would then work on until three or four A.M. When he had finished dictating a speech at three one morning to a bleary-eyed secretary, he remarked, "Don't bother with a fair copy of that tonight.... I shan't want it till eight o'clock."

Churchill was the last true leader Britain ever had—after that, perhaps, Britain did not want or need a leader. Leaders, as opposed to mere political functionaries, inspire whole nations, make them feel and act and function in particular ways. The doggedness, the refusal to give up, the good humor, even the booziness of Londoners at this extraordinary time were reflected in their wartime Prime Minister, whose BBC broadcasts, though an embarrassment to the very sophisticated, held the capital, the nation, and indeed the world in thrall with their bombastic mingling of Macaulay and Gibbon, their iron resolve, and the transparent decency of their philosophy. It was inspired of Margaret Thatcher, when Prime Minister, to open the Cabinet War Rooms and make them into a museum—the map room, with its pins and bits of wool indicating the positions of great armies, the cramped corridors, the rows of telephones, the absolute lack of grandiosity or side, the neatness. It is a place where, you feel, a group of extraordinarily talented and, in the last resort, modest people gathered together to finish a dreadful but vital task, and accomplished it with consummate skill. Whether or not it was Britain's finest hour, it was certainly London's.

12

POSTWAR

The film studios at Ealing Green, West London, were founded in 1931 by Basil Dean, and had helped to establish the cinema careers of George Formby and Gracie Fields. Dean quarreled with his fellow directors and was replaced in 1938 with Michael Balcon, who was in charge of production throughout the war. With backing by Rank and MGM they produced some goodish war films—*London, For Those in Peril*—but it was for the postwar comedies that Ealing Studios became famous, indeed immortal.

Already, by 1954, they were foundering, and they finally closed production in 1957. The films of their glory days, like the 1945–50 Labour government of Clement Attlee, or like the Festival of Britain in 1951, possess an extraordinary quality of their own, depicting an England, and especially a London, which, having come through the war victorious, even triumphant, was at the same time completely vulnerable. Watching these larky black-and-white comedies today, we see an England that was self-mocking, indeed self-parodying. *Kind Hearts and Coronets* is a fantasy in which a man of suburban origins in south London manages, by a series of somehow perfectly harmless-seeming serial murders, to become a duke. (All the aristocratic murder victims are played by Alec Guinness.) In *The Lady Killers* and *The Lavender Hill Mob*, even London's criminal gangs are homely, cheery almost.

The comedy that really began the series and determined the tone of all the rest was the 1949 *Passport to Pimlico*. Now one can watch it for its black-and-white shots of bombed-out streets and a skyline unhaunted by modernist architecture, roads comparatively uncluttered by traffic, tarmac free of road signs or yellow no-parking lines. The eruption of an un-exploded bomb in a small quarter of Pimlico, the district hard by Westminster, reveals hidden treasure, discovered by the local grocer (Stanley Holloway). Thanks to the scholarly evidence of Professor Hatton-Jones (Margaret Rutherford) presented at an inquest, it is discovered that Pimlico, or this small corner of it, belongs, by some ancient charter of Edward IV, to Burgundy, and is therefore technically autonomous. The local bank manager, publican, fishmonger, and friendly policeman join with the grocer to proclaim their independent republic, in which the austerities of the war years and of Attlee's Socialist Britain are done away with in the name of the liberties of old England. There is a liberating scene in which they all tear up their ration books in the pub and toss them in the air like confetti.

At first put out by the rebellion, the Attlee government decides to take them at their word, isolate them with barbed wire, and cut off food and water supplies. The rest of London sympathizes with "plucky little Burgundy." "Don't you know there's a siege on?" asks one of the characters. A parodic Berlin airlift occurs when Londoners bring them food and supplies; and there is a twist ending, when the treasure and gold-rich Pimlico returns to the British fold by lending the bankrupted Socialist Treasury of Stafford Cripps their gold supplies in exchange for various local amenities. The shell hole is filled with clean water for the children to bathe in and becomes the Pimlico Lido. The combination of independent-minded contempt for government bureaucracy with the desire for the social amenities offered by central government foreshadows the "Butskellism" or consensus politics of the 1950s.

If the Ealing comedies produce in the viewer the sense of looking into a vanished age, so, too, does a perusal of the guides and catalogues for the Festival of Britain, 1951. There is such insularity and such optimism.

Britain had held out against the Nazi and Japanese world dominators, held out long enough for the Americans to finish the job by achieving world domination themselves. Both processes—the holding out, and watching America collect the prize—had been isolating in a more than psychological sense. (By the end of the Second World War no banana had been seen in the British Isles for six years.)

In the bleak postwar London depicted by *Passport to Pimlico,* in which much of the city was still scarred by bomb sites and in which rationing continued, the Festival of Britain was conceived as a tonic to the nation. It was planned for 1951, the hundredth anniversary of the Great Exhibition in the Crystal Palace in the middle of Hyde Park, an event had heralded Britain's commercial and political preeminence in the world. The symbol of the festival was a helmeted Britannia of art deco simplicity arising from a star and a sun. The colors of the geometrical borders were red, white, and blue.

The principal London site for the festival exhibition was in the bomb-torn stretch of land between Waterloo Bridge and County Hall. The guiding spirit behind the festival had been Herbert Morrison. The young Hugh Casson was in charge of the design of the site, which used many LCC-employed architects, many artists and designers. The only permanent building on the site was the Royal Festival Hall, a joint effort by a group of LCC architects including, among others, Robert Matthew, Leslie Martin, and Peter Moro. Attending concerts there in the twenty-first century, one feels as if one is stepping into a northern European Socialist world, benign but dull—as it were Trondheim, or Reykjavik. The imperialistic fantasies of Aston Webb, which had produced County Hall, the Admiralty Arch, and the refurbished Buckingham Palace in the Edwardian era only half a century before, had been replaced by a much smaller vision of England as a modest, decent little place, with a pipe-smoking Prime Minister, Mr. Attlee, whose appearance was that of a bank manager or the headmaster of a minor private school.

Whereas the Great Exhibition of 1851, with its Arab, Indian, and other exotic displays, had emphasized the worldwide interests of British commerce and influence, the Festival of Britain tended to celebrate the virtues of Britain. Great emphasis was placed upon town planning and on the housing that would go up to replace the bombed-out old slums.

One of the most eagerly visited parts of the exhibition was a show flat furnished by the London Co-operative Society in close cooperation with the Council of Industrial Design. The modern furniture was easy to clean and affordable. There was an emphasis on living areas being multipurpose—a kitchen-dining-living space being larger, lighter, airier than anything experienced in the little terraces and tenements that most prewar Londoners had known.

Visitors could see plans for the model Lansbury Estate in the East End, and also for such social experiments as the building of Harlow New Town, Essex. A dull but clean paradise opened up for people. Compared with the visitors to the Millennium Dome half a century later, however—that was the brainchild of, among others, Herbert Morrison's grandson Peter Mandelson—the Festival of Britain was a cornucopia of intellectual and visual stimulus. The exhibitions of scientific and engineering achievements, of natural history, of architecture and geology, all presupposed a level of intellectual curiosity, and of information, which was entirely lacking in the various "Zones" of the Mandelson Dome.

This might have been an insular exhibition in some ways, but the visitors were offered, within that limit, an encyclopedic range of useful and interesting information: every species of British bird was either stuffed or constructed out of paper by R. Talbot Kelly. (His eerily accurate paper bird sculptures were indistinguishable from his taxidermy.) The section devoted to the sea told the viewer everything from different species of whales, to shipbuilding, to modern methods of hydrographic survey. A vast exhibition of books at the Victoria and Albert Museum celebrated the literary and bibliopegic skills of the prewar years, before paper shortages put a stop to decent book production. (There were no books visible in the Mandelson Dome.)

———

By the time the exhibition opened, Attlee's Labour administration had been voted out of office and Winston Churchill was once again Prime Minister, to remain so until his retirement, unwillingly reached, in April 1955. He was succeeded by the irascible, sickly, and, as we know now, narcotic-ridden Sir Anthony Eden as Prime Minister.

The Labour Party was voted out of office partly because the electorate was fed up with austerity, but partly because it had won the argument. (Rather in the same way that the electorate dared to vote for Blair's Labour Party in 1997, because it had adopted Thatcherite monetary policies, the electorate of 1951 trusted Churchill once more because he was going to continue the welfare state, the housing program, and the broadly Socialist agenda set out by Attlee, Cripps, and Morrison.)

The determination to rebuild the ravaged capital continued. When the model Lansbury Estate was exhibited in the Festival of Britain, emphasis was placed upon the importance of "neighbourhood." Though the designs of the flats were to be "modern," they should be made to seem familiar by being built from London stock bricks, like the old houses destroyed in the war, and with Welsh slate on the roofs. Schools, markets, pubs, and even churches should be incorporated in the design—the Ricardo Street Primary School, off East India Dock Road, being an example of gentle and not obtrusively or brutally modernistic neighborhood architecture.

In fact, however, although LCC, the City Corporation and the boroughs, and the central government probably all shared the wish to rebuild London in a manner that was humane and decent, they lacked two vital properties: taste and ownership.

First, though there was a natural, fair, and altruistic wish that Londoners, who had endured the Blitz, should to have indoor lavatories and warm sitting rooms, there was no Christopher Wren to oversee the enterprise. In the eighteenth century, had aerial bombardment been a possibility and had London needed to be rebuilt, it would perhaps have mattered less than in the twentieth century, since in that era of architecture, builders and craftsmen were themselves stylists; many of the best eighteenth-century buildings are all but anonymous, put up according to classically tested and approved designs. It so happened that the end of the Second World War coincided with a period of architectural history when these notions had, for reasons that now seem obscure, been rejected by the architectural establishment and when the aesthetic of modernism, largely untried on townscapes in Europe outside the Stalinist satellites, was the inspiring dream of many aspirant practitioners.

But—and this is the second vital fact—even if there had been a Sir Christopher Wren in the era of the Festival of Britain, it is difficult to know how much power he would have had over the rebuilding of postwar London. Strangely enough, the local authorities possessed every legal right to make compulsory purchase of bombed sites—an act of 1944 gave them the right to buy any blitzed areas—but they did not always do so. The war provided the golden opportunity for property developers to acquire acre upon acre of London. The other factor in the fatal story was that many of the old landowners were crushed by the death duties brought in by the Socialist government. For example, in 1953 the death of the second Duke of Westminster cost the Grosvenors £20 million, a bill that could have been covered only by their surrender of Pimlico. True, the big landowners (the Grosvenors, the Cadogans) still owned, and own, huge acreages in London; but in the early 1950s, the clever property developer, having already bought up bomb sites, stood to make more in rents by building high-rise properties than by reproducing the traditional London street patterns. Once planning permission had been granted for one high-rise, the precedent had been established and there was little that could be done to prevent more.

It was, therefore, in the comparatively cozy world of postwar and 1950s London that the decisions were made which would change the London skyline, and the living conditions of Londoners, so irrevocably and with such brutality. When Harold Samuel bought a property company called Land Securities in 1943, "the only real estate of the company now comprises three houses in Kensington, two of which, the directors regret to state, are unoccupied." Twenty-five years later, the assets of Land Securities, Limited, amounted to £28 million. Harry Hyams, the doyen of developers, took over Oldham Estates at £22,328 in 1959.[1] By 1967, it was worth £46 million.

In the late 1950s, the LCC wanted to build a large motor roundabout at the intersection of Tottenham Court Road and Oxford Street. The land was owned by Pearlmans, directors of the Ve-ri Best Manufacturing Company, which was in fact not a manufacturing company at all but a property company. They turned down an offer of £55,000 for Ve-ri Best. But then along came Harry Hyams, who bought out Pearlmans for half a million, acquired several adjacent properties, then rented back the land on a lease to the LCC at £18,500 per annum. In the middle of the site, Hyams proposed to erect a thirty-five story office block. There was still on the statute books the 1939 London Building Act, which forbade buildings of more than a hundred feet, but this contained the deadly loophole "unless the Council otherwise consent."

Since the council were in Hyams's debt, they could hardly refuse his desire to build Centre Point, which was completed in 1967. Construction costs were about £3.5 million. The finished building was "worth" some £17 million, a net profit of £11 million simply through the rise in property prices. Hyams nevertheless left the building empty for years to await the rise in rentals. The LCC never actually built their roundabout. There Centre Point stands, a monument to greed and folly, a perpetual obstruction, since there is no decent sidewalk around it and anyone who alights from a bus in New Oxford Street near its base has to weave a circuitous course by crossing three or four roads if he wishes to get to the top of Charing Cross Road.

The architect of Centre Point was Richard Seifert, an undistinguished figure whose architectural experience was limited in prewar days to minor domestic projects in north London. He once won second prize for designing a boring façade for the Building Centre, Store Street, off Tottenham Court Road. Seifert's genius was not for architecture, as Londoners are now all too painfully aware: it was for getting round planning regulations. This made him the ideal man for Harry Hyams, who commissioned him to design the thirty-six fin-shaped stories of Centre Point. He was to go on to design the NatWest Tower, opened in 1981 but already condemned then as obsolescent and reminiscent of the 1960s, at the time the tallest unbraced building in the world, each of its fifty office floors bringing in huge rentals for the property company. He built high-rise flats in Birmingham and Glasgow, but it is in London that he made his mark: the Kensington Palace Hotel blights Kensington Gardens just as Tolworth House, all twenty-two stories of it, influenced by the Brazilian expressionist Oscar Niemeyer, looms out of scale over Kingsway. "Seifert," said his obituary in the *Guardian* in October 2001, "built more London buildings than Sir Christopher Wren and undeniably had as great an effect upon the city skyline."

Seifert, of course, was not alone. The Corporation of London, somewhat unwillingly at first, were urged by the LCC to take over the forty-acre bomb site of the Barbican and to create there a complex of flats, theaters, and other amenities. The only building within that site to survive bombardment is St. Giles Cripplegate, the church where Milton was buried. The brutalist result, rough-hewn and threatening, looms out of a chaos of swirling roads. Finding your way in or out as a pedestrian or a motorist is a hazardous undertaking. Few now can consider the Barbican Centre an object of beauty.

When asked to redesign the Royal College of Physicians, next to the Nash terraces in Regent's Park, Denys Lasdun in 1959 came up with a poor imitation of Le Corbusier. The academic world was so impressed by the unsparing results that Lasdun was asked to rebuild the School of Oriental and African Studies in Bloomsbury, and the University of East Anglia. Hungry for more disproportionately massive flat layers of concrete, those anxious for a National Theatre invited him to adorn the banks of the Thames with his protuberant oblongs.

As these masterpieces of twentieth-century taste rose before the eyes of Londoners, the government commissioned Basil Spence to design a tower block for Knightsbridge Barracks (approved 1960, built 1967).

Lasdun's public or university buildings might now seem good for a laugh, but imagine having to live in the cluster block he designed in Claredale Street, Bethnal Green, which towers over the attractively proportioned old tenement buildings. "Lasdun," writes an admirer, "was given the opportunity to explore some of his ideas in reality in the early 1950s."[2]

The cluster was perhaps preferable to the truly high-rise blocks into which Londoners, usually the poorer Londoners, were herded by housing authorities in the 1950s and 1960s. Students of architecture claim that Ernö Goldfinger's Trellick Tower in north Kensington is an object of beauty, but most people must see it as a blight, an affront to any of the ideals so touchingly expressed by the Festival of Britain.

We have dwelt at length upon architecture, since it is the dominant fact of postwar London: the city had to be rebuilt somehow, and it happened to be rebuilt in a particular way. But the 1950s were also an era of growing prosperity. The Port of London had been patched up and by mid-decade it was still the largest employer of manpower in the capital, with a thousand ships docked there each week. The industries of the suburbs were productive as never before. The London aircraft industry—Vickers at Weybridge, Surrey; Viscount at Colindale, just west of Hendon—enjoyed a golden age, with Hatfield de Haviland producing the world's first jet airliner, the Comet.

At Dagenham, Essex, Ford were producing 250,000 cars a year. All this was going to change at the beginning of the sixties; but even after the debacle of Suez in 1956, when Eden resigned to be replaced by Macmillan, it was by no means clear to most Londoners that Britain's place in the world, and its very identity, had irrevocably altered.

Londoners could believe Harold Macmillan's smug political slogan that they had "never had it so good." If this was true for the law-abiding, it was by extension good for the criminals, since at last there was some money to steal after the austerity years. Wage snatches, of a kind parodied in the Ealing

Comedy *The Lavender Hill Mob,* became the vogue, with Billy Town's Camden Town mob getting away with £287,000 in cash after one raid on a post office van in Eastcastle Street, Marylebone. Blaggings, as the friendly homegrown Cockney criminals called robberies of this kind, increased in London by 68 percent between 1955 and 1957. Charlie and Eddie Richardson ran one of the most ruthless of south London protection rackets. Ronnie and Reggie Kray, twins from Bethnal Green (born 1933) specialized in protection rackets and gaming clubs, where they could enjoy the pleasures of extortion, torture, and robbery, and add the pleasures of social climbing. They enjoyed being photographed with such figures as Judy Garland, George Raft (himself linked with the Mafia), and Lord Boothby, the notorious bisexual lover of the Prime Minister's wife, Lady Dorothy Macmillan.

Boothby's link with the Bethnal Green gangster world was a sexual one, but it was one of those satisfying reminders of how London links up by tenuous threads of cognition and acquaintanceship, and how the crimes of the poor and those of the rich interlace. Just as highway robbery flourished at the beginning of banks and stockbroking, in the reign of Queen Anne, it seems apt that in the era of Supermac (Harold Macmillan), property speculation and protection racketeering should have become chief among London's trades. They had never had it so good. So it would seem if you look at Dan Farson's photographs of bohemian life in Soho bars, or read Iris Murdoch's racy novels of adultery and homosexuality in London's arty world.

After the heroic years of war, and the necessity for everyone to pull together and behave well, there was a palpable and collective need to behave badly, or at least to seem to behave badly. In 1955 the police made a raid on the legendary Fitzroy Tavern in north Soho. They found between fifty and eighty people who "paraded themselves unashamedly" with "rouged" cheeks and "blatantly dyed" hair. Constable Pyle said in his evidence that he had been approached by a prostitute who had asked, with a winsome smile, "Are you looking for a naughty girl or a naughty boy?"[3] The decades to come would demonstrate that London had plenty of both to choose from, and that the police could do very little to stop them.

13

THE END
OF THE
BOWLER HAT

Even until the late 1960s or early 1970s, if you stood on the platform of a suburban or provincial railway station in England it was possible to identify those male passengers who were going up to London. They were the ones wearing bowler hats. When Peter Walker finished his National Service in the 1950s, he was offered a position as an insurance broker in the City firm of Griffiths Tate. "You will be joining the American Department on 1 May," the letter of appointment informed him. "Your salary will be £300 per annum, your hours of work will be 8.45 a.m. to 5.30 p.m. Monday to Friday and 8.45 to 12 noon on Saturday. You will have two weeks' holiday a year. You will wear a bowler hat to and from the office."[1]

Thousands, tens of thousands, of office workers in the civil service, and in journalism and the City, were clad in almost identical clothes—dark suit, bowler, a furled umbrella on the arm. By the 1970s such figures would look old-fashioned. By the 1980s, for a man under fifty to wear a bowler hat would look positively bizarre. The outfit proclaimed an inner self-picture. The various workplaces of London—the Bar, the City, and even to a certain extent the journalistic fraternity of Fleet Street—were all seen as institutions, almost as clubs to whose rule a chap—and it was very much a male world—was expected to conform.

The efficiency and wealth-creating capacity of the City actually depended upon the brokers and dealers all belonging, in fact, and not just in theory, to a cohesive social group. The smaller merchant banks and investment companies, the family-run insurance businesses, the stockbroking firms were all permeated with varying types of social glue, which enabled the chaps to stick together and to know "who anyone was." There were the private schools at which the richer chaps had all been educated. There were the clubs to which they belonged, and there were the livery companies by which the institutions of the City were administered. There were the old families, still dominant in the City.

"Hallo, Jacob, what are you up to these days?" the journalist Paul Foot breezily asked of his old Oxford acquaintance Rothschild, when they bumped into one another in the 1960s.

"I work at the bank which bears my name" was the reply.

Your Hambros, your Barings, your Cattos and Cazenoves, were the aristocracy of the City, but there was an army of well-heeled lesser beings, all of whom were in the club together. Jiggery-pokery was not their aim: it was too obviously not in their interest. They wished to become richer, but to do so honestly and with "sound money."

But different times lay ahead. The Big Bang in the City on October 27, 1986, took account of the new technology. It was now possible to buy and sell shares other than on the floor of the London Stock Exchange. The chaps, in their paneled boardrooms, clubhouses, and City halls, would really have no control anymore over who was going to be buying and selling. Many of those who rose to prominence in the new, fast-moving world of finance were fast-living spivs who certainly had not been to university with anyone famous and assuredly did not have banks bearing their own name. Tim Congdon, in an article in *The Spectator* a week before the Big Bang, pointed out,

> It is a sideshow to, indeed almost a by-product of, a much Bigger Bang which has transformed international finance over the last 25 years. This Bigger Bang bears about the same

relation to the Big Bang as the construction of Canary Wharf to the refurbishment of the Royal Exchange. One totally over-shadows and dwarfs the other. Whereas the Bigger Bang is a new departure in the pattern of international financial activity, the Big Bang merely alters the way in which a long established business is conducted.[2]

The collapse in 1995 of Barings Bank, an impeccable blameless enterprise for 105 years, was a parable of what was happening to the City of London, likened by William Rees-Mogg to the sinking of the *Hood* in the Second World War. The twenty-eight-year-old trader who appeared to bring about the collapse single-handed was Nick Leeson, born in a council house in Watford, whose mysterious activities in front of a computer screen in Singapore managed to clock up astounding losses, hundreds of millions. But it would be a very simple-minded diehard who supposed that Nick Leeson's story merely showed what happened when you let a chap into the club who wasn't quite the thing. The *Sunday Times* remarked, as Barings went down:

> In layman's terms, Barings' top team chose to smash through red light after red light in a craven chase for "easy" profits. Then, in the final moments, when it was clear that the next stop was a brick wall, they scrambled desperately to find someone, anyone other than themselves to blame. Leeson, the oik from Watford, looked the perfect fall-guy.

The truth is that in the heyday of Margaret Thatcher and Thatcherism, when there was no such thing as society, everyone, and not just the Baring family, was addicted to the idea that work was a thing of the past. Money could be made by magic. The yuppies or slickers who knew how to operate the arcane mysteries of the computer and the markets they seemed to control could make sums of money of which earlier generations had not even dreamed.

Everyone in London was affected by the dream: it was as though a collective South Sea Bubble had taken hold of London's imagination. The City itself might contain old-fashioned men, who had first gone to work wearing bowler hats, who now deplored what was happening, but they were powerless, as Swiss Bank Corporation took over Warburgs, Kleinwort Benson were taken over by Dresdner Bank, and all the great British merchant banks, some of which had been in business on the same site since the reign of William III, fell to foreign and collective ownership. (As the sentence implies, England itself had done quite well out of Dutch takeover all those years back.)

It was easy to speak sentimental words about the good old days, but the power of the market, in the short term, to make Londoners rich was like a drug. Londoners watched their flats and houses double and quadruple in price, and then double again. Writers, who had been paid a few hundred pounds for their books, suddenly found that publishing could be treated like any other industry, with huge sums paid for the takeovers and conglomerations, and concomitant riches offered to them. The managers and editors who attempted to make the account books balance had as much chance of doing so as Swift's academician, attempting to extract sunbeams from cucumbers.[3]

Old London had been a workplace in which the leisured classes were in the minority. New London became a playground, where those who worked, in any of the recognizable meanings of the term, were hugely outnumbered by those seeking leisure, thrill, gratification. The London of the last forty years has grown steadily richer than it has been at any period in its history. The value of property has increased often and by vast dimensions. Every time there is a boom in the property market, a minority get trapped. They have over-borrowed; for a short period their property is worth less than they paid for it, and they are the victims of "negative equity." Yet pass a number of years, and the same property will once more have multiplied in value.

This roller-coaster economy, in which the flat or house in which a Londoner lives becomes his or her chief asset, has produced the peculiar mixture of angst and idleness that characterizes modern London. Everyone worries, if they are a property owner, that they can't afford their mortgage. Yet they know that if they can only hold on to paid employment of some kind, their little nest egg will make them feel rich. The studio flat bought for £23,000 in 1978 was worth £122,000 in 1999; the terraced house bought for £350,000 in 1997 is worth over £1 million in 2004. Those who can't assemble enough money to put down a deposit for a flat or a house merely look around for some other means of getting a roof over their heads. Council-owned accommodation is of enormously varied quality, some grotty, some perfectly all right. If you are never going to be able to earn enough to become a mortgage slave, why save? Earn, or get hold of, enough to pay the essentials and spend the rest.

If you walk about London any part of London, rich or poor on a weekday in 2003, the immediate thing to strike you is that most of the population are not really working. Many of them are shopping. Many are sitting around in cafés or bars. In post offices there are long queues. Less than a tenth of the people in the queue are waiting to post a parcel. Most are queuing for money which they draw out. An old-fashioned person noting the extraordinary idleness of Londoners might very well be shocked, and would hark back in a spirit of nostalgia to the time when the docks employed tens of thousands of toiling stevedores, lightermen, ferrymen, and dockers; when all over

London small factories and businesses required the actual physical labor of those with the skill to make motors, pianos, candlesticks, watches, shirts, or vinegar.

In fact, all the fastest-growing London-based businesses in the last twenty years of the twentieth century were posited on the sociological fact that work, as understood by our ancestors, was now very largely unnecessary. Sandwich bars, record shops, cheap but fashionable clothes shops, bars, restaurants, hotels, private art galleries, nightclubs for the young and the very young—these were the things that made entrepreneurs rich in the period 1965–2003. These and the trade in illegal drugs, which were used by a majority of Londoners under the age of twenty.

When the Swinging Sixties began the economy of London, seeming to rely on its docks and manufacturing, looked as if it were in terminal decline. When long haired drug-taking pop musicians made recordings at Abbey Road in St. John's Wood, it might have seemed to the diehards as if they were the last nail in civilization's coffin. Perhaps they were, but the Beatles and the Rolling Stones, while making themselves immensely rich, also stimulated the economy more than a hundred factories of Old Cockney Tyme making coffee essence or boot blacking. The London working classes produced a galaxy of figures in the 1960s destined to stimulate the economy in comparable ways with film, music, fashion, or chic: the photographer David Bailey, from East Ham, Terence Stamp, Michael Caine, all the Rolling Stones, all the Who, Adam Faith, Helen Shapiro, and countless others. It was noted that when the Beatles appeared on the balcony of Liverpool Town Hall after the world premiere of *A Hard Day's Night* in 1964, they did not stay for the reception given by their friendly fellow scousers but returned instantly to London, which had made them and where all their best recordings were done.[4]

The something-for-nothing approach, which appeared to

enrich shareholders and slickers, could hardly fail to infect those nominally opposed to capitalism, for you cannot touch pitch and not be tarred. The perky leader of the Greater London Council introduced a "low fare initiative," Just the Ticket and Fares Fair, forcing London Transport to cut their costs and yet providing no obvious means to pay for such munificence. During the operation of Fares Fair in 1982, there was a 6 percent drop in cars during the rush hour. There were many who saw the GLC leader, Ken Livingstone, as something of a hero. But London politics had, at least since Victorian times, always been riven with party interests and mixed motives. It is hard to see Livingstone in his GLC manifestation, with his desire to abolish the ancient mayoralty and corporation of the City, as a great benefactor to London. Compare the houses, flats, and parks (including Hampstead Heath—administered by the Corporation of London) with the filthy, rundown, and ill-funded equivalents administered either by the GLC or the boroughs.

The Greater London Council came into being in 1965. The London Government Act of 1963 extended the jurisdiction of the old London County Council but created, if anything, more muddle than existed before—with, for example, transport policy in the control of at least three often opposing powers. The boroughs took charge of road maintenance; the GLC was responsible for parking policy; but for larger trunk roads in and around the capital the Department of Transport in central government retained responsibility. In housing, there were comparable bureaucratic entanglements, with boroughs and central government vying with the GLC to blame one another for the appalling design and inadequate provision of housing. Conservatives were pleased to point out that the GLC and Labour boroughs wasted money and charged higher rates than Tory boroughs. The GLC wanted to put money into subsidizing fringe theater and ephemeral fashion projects, while offering no contribution of note to the capital's opera houses or orchestras. The Victorian Conservatives under Lord Salisbury had delighted in the prospect of the boroughs being at loggerheads with a liberal LCC. By the 1980s, the Labour Party was supposedly in the grip of "extremists." The Limehouse Declaration, issued from the East End residence of a former Labour Foreign Secretary, David Owen, formed the Social Democratic Party. It was initially attractive to those who felt that the Labour Party was turning Trotskyite, and Livingstone, always a showman more than a substantial political figure, allowed the Conservatives to represent him as the extremist. With very little fuss, Mrs. Thatcher's government abolished the GLC altogether, and County Hall, that architectural embodiment of London's civic hopes, was put up for sale. The advertisements called it "London's most exciting real estate opportunity."

The Conservatives and the Socialists in both central and local government signally failed to provide London with efficient government. In the Thatcher era the largest and richest city in Europe contained, in such boroughs as Tower Hamlets, some of the poorest urban areas. The problem of homelessness spilled onto the streets, so that Lasdun's brutalist structure of theaters and walkways on the South Bank became "Cardboard City," a shantytown. This almost Peruvian spectacle was in easy sight of the childish production-line modernist structures in the City, where the slickers were making their bonuses of £1 million a year.

Poverty on the scale which London had known in the early years of the twentieth century did not return. But the gap between rich and poor grew larger, leaving more reason, and some would think justification, for the unemployable, ill-educated poor to believe that the only natural reaction to their plight was crime. Many—through whose fault it is perhaps vain to speculate—found themselves in a "poverty trap," where the mental work they might find would pay less than the benefit they would receive for being unemployed. Some would blame this on the dependency culture created by a too-liberal system of state welfare, others by a failure of imagination by governments and employers to find young people suitable occupations or employment. A generation was growing up who had known nothing of the system of apprenticeship, in an economy that was no longer dependent either on manufacturing industry or, much, upon manual labor. Those children, born on the modernist council estates of Tottenham, Catford, or Staines, sent to badly run comprehensive schools and offered no hope or encouragement of work, were not poor as those in a Victorian workhouse, nor as those on the Jarrow Hunger March were poor. But at least the poor of an earlier age could hope for the narcotic of manual labor, rather than being lured into the narcotics for sale on the London street, such as crack cocaine and heroin, substances that once tried could be hard to put down; and once adopted as a habit might require the habit of violent crime to sustain.

A good number of people caught by the poverty trap were those of white parentage. But it was only to be expected, given the socioeconomic structure of London in this period, that a high proportion of those who found themselves out of work and drifting into crime should have been black.

Much of the cheap journalism and neo-Fascist propaganda which dwells on this phenomenon draws the easy conclusion that young black males have a natural propensity to violent crime. Do not the statistics speak for themselves? Are not the majority of street crimes, the majority of muggings, committed by young males of Afro-Caribbean or African extraction, chiefly the former? To attribute a racial cause to the criminality of young London blacks is a little like suggesting that Filipino women have a racially inbuilt obsession with domestic drudgery, which draws them to badly paid work in

European hotels, or that Thai children recruited into prostitution to service sex tourists are innately lascivious. By contrast, it could be seen that all these young people are the products of economic and political situations over which they have no control. London has been a useful place to observe the late-twentieth-century phenomenon of racial mixing and migration. Much of what has happened there has challenged stereotypical prejudice.

14

LONDON
COSMOPOLIS

I am writing this in the afternoon of a typical London day. I deposit my daughter at school with her Mexican classroom assistant and her friends whose parents are, to name but seven, Italian, African American, Japanese, Chinese, Palestinian, German, and Indian. Having left my daughter at school, where the janitor is an Ethiopian, I return home to let in a Sikh furniture upholsterer. (He and his father have worked up such a successful business in Kentish Town that they have managed to build a fine family house in the hills of the Punjab.) Saying hello to my Brazilian cleaning lady, I make for the local Italian café for breakfast, then on the British Library where two African women and a Cypriot check my pass, and where a variety of excellent and helpful library clerks man the Issue and Return desk. Today, they consist of two West Indians, an Italian, and several different African nationalities as well as white English. A Malaysian cuts my hair. Then I have lunch at the Travellers' Club, where my meal is brought to me by a friendly Bulgarian, my wine by a Frenchwoman, and my coffee by an Egyptian. I go home on a Tube train driven by a Trinidadian, buy my copy of the evening paper from a Pakistani corner shop, pick up my dry cleaning from the Irish family who run Paradise Dry Cleaning, Park Way, and buy my bottle of hooch from the Irish man and woman who run the local off-license. I pop into the local bookshop, run by refugees from Hitler's Vienna and their son, say hello to some neighbors—one white Zimbabwean, another American married to a Greek—and I go home. Bogdan, a Polish carpenter, comes to discuss rebuilding some shelves that were put up in our kitchen by a cowboy English builder. Since we have a baby-sitter tonight, my wife and I then debate whether to eat at our local Italian or Indian restaurant or whether to go a little farther afield and try a new Russian place that sounds interesting.

Every single person I have met today is a Londoner, and I do not feel that they are foreign to the city any more than I am myself, having migrated here like thousands before me from a provincial boyhood.

In April 1968, a former Conservative Health Minister, J. Enoch Powell, made a speech in Birmingham that was to reverberate through the later decades of the twentieth century in Britain. He called for an immediate end to the flow of immigrants into the United Kingdom and proposed a policy of "re-emigration" to the countries of the British Commonwealth whence the immigrants had come—the Caribbean, Bangladesh, Pakistan and India, as well as a variety of African countries. He said that to allow fifty thousand immigrants and their dependents each year into Britain was mad: "It is like watching a nation busily engaged in heaping up its own funeral pyre." And, with an allusion to the Cumaean Sibyl in the sixth book of the *Aeneid,* he said that he saw the Tiber foaming with much blood.

Within days, the leader of the Conservative Party, Edward Heath, had sacked Powell from the shadow cabinet and Enoch had become a working-class hero among such unlikely figures as the Communist dockers. On April 23, St. George's Day, these patriots, who had all but ruined the London docks by their persistent strikes and outlandish pay demands, decided that the real reason for the ending of over nine hundred years of successful trading in the port was immigration. In St. Katherine's Dock, two thousand men went on strike and marched on Westminster brandishing banners to tell the world that Enoch was right. When they reached the Commons, they swarmed into the central lobby, where a mustachioed buffoon by the name of Sir Gerald Nabarro MP (a good old English name) received rousing cheers for telling them of his support for Enoch's views.

Yet it is now the twenty-first century and the Tiber, by which one can only assume Powell meant the Thames, is not foaming with blood. Panic, largely based on the color of the new immigrants' skin, has characterized British responses to demographic change in the last fifty years of London's history. When SS *Windrush* docked at Tilbury on June 22, 1948, and 492 individuals from the Caribbean stepped onto British soil (most of them to settle in Brixton, south London), a spokesman for the Colonial Office said, "This unorganized rush is a disaster. We knew nothing about it." By the mid-fifties Caribbean immigrants were coming into London at the rate of about a thousand a year, but only about a third settled in the capital. There were around twenty thousand in the mid-fifties and by 1961 nearly a hundred thousand had entered Britain. Inevitably, there was some racist response, most notably in Notting Hill, where in the hot summer of 1958, crowds of up to seven hundred "Teddy boys" and a few older Fascist diehards had attacked the black people living in poor lodging houses of north Kensington.

In 1981, on April 10–12, there were riots in Brixton when young black people clashed with police after what was perceived as clumsy policing and the crowd believed, falsely, that a police officer had stabbed a youth. The looting and burning that followed were hardly comparable with the Gordon Riots, but the disturbances were enough to cause serious alarm. The Archbishop of Canterbury, Dr. Robert Runcie, who had been at Oxford in the Conservative Club with the Prime Minister, Margaret Thatcher, annoyed her by suggesting that these riots were not merely racial in flavor but reflected a sense of frustration among young people in a deprived inner-city area where prospects of employment were low.

In September 1985 there were more disturbances in Brixton when Mrs. Cherry Groce was shot by the police using a Smith & Wesson .38. The damage done was estimated at £3 million. A week later, in a hideous housing estate at Broadwater Farm in Tottenham, north London (a housing development that had won prizes for the Haringey Architects Department that designed it in 1971, but that was now barely habitable), the police raided a suspected criminal's home. Mrs. Cynthia Jarrett suffered a fatal heart attack during the police search, and fires broke out all over the development. A much loved local police constable named Blakelock was attacked by an angry mob. He died after being stabbed more than forty times with knives and machetes. Someone was heard calling for him to be beheaded.

At ten-thirty P.M. on Thursday, April 22, 1993, an eighteen-year-old black boy, Stephen Lawrence, was murdered on the corner of Well Hall Road and Dickson Road, Eltham. He had apparently been killed by a gang of five or six white youths and the motive for the murder appeared to be racial. A black friend was also injured. Stephen had been a studious, peaceable young man, hoping to study architecture. His parents achieved national, indeed international, renown for the persistence with which they attempted to pursue justice on his behalf. No one was prosecuted for his murder, and in all the subsequent inquiries the Metropolitan Police went through a perhaps overdue spell of self-reproach for its "institutional racism."

None of these things—the Notting Hill riots, the Brixton riots, the disturbances on the Broadwater Farm Estate, or the murder of Stephen Lawrence—is to be taken lightly. Yet the very fact that these incidents are rehearsed in the annals of London history is surely itself significant. The truth is that for the most part London has not foamed with blood or crackled with flames. It has been largely peaceable. The racism, institutional or otherwise, of the white population has not been comparable with that of the Ku Klux Klan, and most prophecies of disaster have been unfounded.

But mass immigration has undoubtedly changed London's character and it has created problems. Enoch Powell himself, when he was Health Minister, described the National Health Service as "the envy of the world." He also, at that stage of his career, liked the idea of identifying the British and Roman empires. It pleased him, as a classical scholar, to think of the inhabitants of Nigeria or Jamaica or Pakistan being able to say "Civis Romanus sum." It also pleased him, when he was a health minister with a shortage, even in those days, of doctors and nurses and hospital orderlies and cleaners, to import these from the former dominions and colonies.

It would be true to say that the National Health hospitals in London, the buses, and the Underground trains would all have ceased to operate decades ago were it not for the willingness of immigrant workers and their descendants to work for low wages. Here, however, the immigrant groups divide very much along lines of national origin and economic circumstance. Among the Chinese, the Indians and Pakistanis, the African Asians, and many of the West Africans, especially Ghanaians and Nigerians, there has been a large measure of success in worldly, economic terms. These have followed the pattern set by previous immigrant groups, the Jews of the 1930s or late Victorian era, the Huguenots of the early eighteenth century: they arrived in poverty, but they have made a success of some business or another and thereby enriched not only themselves but London itself.

The case has been otherwise among Afro-Caribbean families. Many of them came to work in such poorly paid jobs as nurses, bus conductors, cleaners. Their immigration coincided with a period when the postwar boom was over and unemployment was rising. This was especially so in London. Partly because of world trade, partly because of the decline in national fortune, the London docks began to close; their demise was, as we have said, greatly hastened by the shortsighted wage demands of the all-white dockers. East India Dock, which closed in 1967, St. Katherine's, and finally London Dock simply could not compete with Rotterdam or Dunkirk. (A mere 10.5 million tons of cargo was handled by the Port of London in the year 2000, a fraction of what passed through in its heyday.) London's manufacturing industry, in common with that of the nation as a whole, began to be drastically reduced, to the point where it would effectually evaporate.

What, then, was a Caribbean young man to do at such a period? Ethnic groups help their own, not merely by employing them but by offering role models and examples. The child of the poor Jewish tailor in Stepney in the 1920s could dream of owning a suburban villa in Stanmore like his rich cousins, if he had the right breaks. Similar dreams might stabilize and give momentum to the life of the poor Pakistani youth whose uncle had made it big in computers, or the Bangladeshi with a chain of restaurants, starting in Brick Lane and ending up in the West End. Enoch Powell unpleasantly predicted in 1968 that within a few generations the "black man would have the whip hand over the white man." Nothing could have turned out to be further from the truth, with economic and educational opportunities slipping from the grasp of black boys stuck in the poverty trap created partly by an appalling educational system, partly by the dependency culture resultant on benefits, partly by an ever burgeoning drug culture.

Certainly, it is all a very long way from *Passport to Pimlico.* As we have already observed, that film represented a particularly uncharacteristic phase of London's history when, thanks to the Second World War and in spite of an influx of Hitler's refugees, it had lost much of its cosmopolitan richness and variety. For an older generation, mass immigration was a difficult phenomenon to observe. Few white people, if they were honest with themselves, did not read of the murder of Police Constable Blakelock on the Broadwater Farm Estate without allowing, with however small a part of their psyche, the idea to form in their heads that something "primitive" had happened, that black people were now showing their true colors. The murder of Stephen Lawrence eight years later, tragic as it was, caused many white people to recognize that "savagery" was not the preserve of one ethnic group or another.

Some of the neo-Fascist fringe might speak of "repatriating" black or Asian people to their grandparents' country of origin, but most Londoners of whatever background recognize that all has changed, that in many respects it has changed for the better, and that this "better" extends beyond a wider availability of curry houses. Yet the fortress mentality is hard to shake off entirely. Migration Watch UK, a newish group led by a former diplomat and an Oxford University demographer, predicts that 2 million people will arrive in the UK every ten years for the foreseeable future. There has been a very dramatic increase in the population of the UK since the late 1990s with, proportionally, an almost identical increase in the crime rate. It would seem that 125,000 new immigrants settled in the UK in 2002.[1]

The great proportion of asylum seekers, legal or illegal, gravitate towards London, because that is where they can hope to find work and where they can most easily lose themselves in a crowd. The population, which has been growing since 1989, is expected to reach 8.1 million by 2016, 700,000 more than it is today.[2]

How you react to all these facts and figures will very largely depend on your temperament. London could never have stayed still after the Second World War. Given Britain's imperial past and its liberal attitudes, on which it had prided itself, to travelers, refugees, and foreign visitors, and given the invention of airplanes and airports, it was inevitable that huge numbers of people from different parts of the world would have wished to come and take up residence in London. Heathrow Airport opened as London Airport in 1946, Gatwick in 1958, and Stansted in 1964. Since London no longer has a manufacturing economy, it depends more and more on the thousands who pour in, most of them tourists, bringing the chief source of revenue for many restaurants, hotels, and entertainers.

London is now a town much more like New York than it is like Rome or Paris. It does not have a particularly national identity. The big City institutions are largely staffed, funded, and run, as well as owned, by hugely powerful non-British companies, American, German, and Japanese. The economy depends upon non-British holidaymakers coming in huge numbers to be fed and tended by, on the whole, non-British restaurateurs, hoteliers, entertainers, prostitutes, and the like. Meanwhile, the great majority of ordinary workers in London cannot afford to live within twenty miles of its center and must commute to work using the increasingly unsatisfactory public transport systems.

15

SILLY LONDON

The history of London does not stop; but any book hoping to chronicle that history must do so. Freeze. Stop the camera. Capture the moment—now, of the London where I sit, in the January of 2003. In the issue of the *Independent* for Wednesday, January 22, are two articles that in very different ways capture contemporary London.

The first, by Johann Hari, is entitled "What I Discovered inside Finsbury Park Mosque." It is an extraordinary piece of prose. Most of the Londoners described in this book—Pepys, Dr. Johnson, Henry Mayhew, Herbert Morrison—might, were they to read it, have wondered whether it was a work of fiction. Edward Gibbon, who described the defeat of the Saracens by Charles Martel in the fifty-second chapter of his great history, pointed out that if that eighth-century military victory had not taken place, "perhaps the interpretation of the Koran would now be taught in the schools of Oxford, and her pulpits might demonstrate to a circumcised people the sanctity and truth of the revelation of Mahomet."[1] Gibbon would have looked with a sardonic eye on the story told by Mr. Hari, who, by virtue of having "a vaguely Islamic-sounding name (in fact Swiss)" and having studied Islamic philosophy at university, "and because I look about 12 years old," found his way into the mosque in the north London suburb of Finsbury Park. It was a place built in the 1990s at the prompting of the Prince of Wales, in the hopes that it would provide a recreational, educational, and social center for the many young Muslims living in the area. It was, from the late 1990s onwards, quickly taken over by extremists; the figure of Abu Hamza, with his one eye and his hook instead of a hand, became a familiar bogeyman in tabloid newspapers in the aftermath of September 11, 2001. Johann Hari is struck, in his article, by the violence of the gender politics that obsess the young men of this mosque. They hate the "sluttish" way that London women dress: "We allow all our women to be whores, dirty fucking whores." Hari reports that "no conversation would go by for five minutes without returning to this topic. These are, after all, sexually frustrated young men who are convinced that even masturbation is immoral—so, like all people who fanatically suppress their sexuality, they have begun to hate the thing they desire."

Abu Hamza, the Captain Hook to these lost boys, feeds their minds with what Hari calls "theocratic fascism." Yet when the police raided the mosque, finding there a number of items that troubled the security forces, Johann Hari could not help feeling a "slight tinge of sadness." "Shorn of Hamza, shorn of the handful of lunatic preachers who gravitate towards it, the mosque has the potential to be a terrific community centre for local Muslims, as mosques across the Arab world are."

Optimists will believe that all the mosques in London, which are growing in number, will provide a similar refuge and inspiration in very confused times. London, which has seen the fires of Smithfield, when a Catholic queen burnt Protestant heretics, and the fires of the Gordon Riots, when a mob attacked Catholics at the end of the eighteenth century, is no stranger to religious bigotry. And yet it is hard not to feel that, when the bigotry is non-Christian, a new phase has been entered.

In the same issue of the *Independent*, another young writer, Jemima Lewis, editor of *The Week*, began an article with the words "London is under attack." She was not referring to a terrorist threat, but to the "doom-sayers" who believe that London transport doesn't work, and that its crime and squalor are out of control. Miss Lewis disagrees:

> Far from going to the dogs, London is better than ever. Once famous for its filthy food, stinking air, blackened buildings and atmosphere of defeat, it is now a neon-lit and cosmopolitan place of beauty. If you doubt me, walk across Waterloo Bridge at night. The banks of the Thames—for so long dark and neglected—are now ablaze with light. The futuristic pods of the London Eye, the golden silhouette of the Houses of Parliament, the glowing red sign of the Oxo tower, the blinking lights of faraway sky-scrapers, and the pale silvery dome of St Paul's: London, which always lacked a proper nocturnal skyline, now has one of the most ravishing in the world.

Jemima Lewis says that fifty years ago London was a parochial city of bad food and gloomy attitudes, but has now become "a city of pleasure.... Every evening after work, thousands of grey commuters tear off their suits and gyrate wildly at salsa clubs and belly-dancing classes. We've come a long way since the demise of the bowler hat."

Both these journalistic snapshots of London at the beginning of the twenty-first century are accurate. On the one hand, the capital city is a place where Islam is making more impact, in many respects, than Christianity and where growing numbers of young people feel not merely disillusionment with, but violent hatred of, everything to do with their fellow citizens. The young people crowding into bars and salsa clubs whom Miss Lewis finds such a cheering prospect are anathema to the fanatics of Finsbury Park. We all know now what a potentially explosive thing that is.

The lights of London make it look pretty at night but even the sunny Miss Lewis would probably agree that much of modern London looks hideous by day, especially by wet day. The M11 swooping and snarling into the North Circular Road from the east, the M1 crunching into Finchley from the north, the Westway swooping across west London to the chaos of Shepherd's Bush, all clogged with lorries and cars belching their noxious exhaust fumes—these are not a cheering sight. And only the most romantic optimist would find much to delight the eye in the huge sprawl of roads and ugly modern buildings south of the river. The graffiti-sprayed council estates that litter the suburban outskirts are nurseries of vice and crime. The bus services are badly organized. The funding and organization of the Underground service are scandalously inadequate.

Yet there are a few exceptions even to these gloomy observations. After generations of boring architecture, the Jubilee Line extension has commissioned Underground stations where space, light, perspective, and line are at last recovered. The new Westminster station by Michael Hopkins and Partners, Waterloo by Sui Te Wu and team, Southwark by Richard MacCormac, and London Bridge by Andrew Weston and Chris Williamson are all outstanding. Canary Wharf, by Foster and Partners, ceased to be a station and became an imitation airport, its seemingly endless escalators swooping the ever growing number of office workers who commute to that part of London (more than 25,000 daily) into a garishly lit array of shopping malls that could be anywhere.

If Canary Wharf is a fantasy airport, the journey to the real Heathrow, one of the most tedious features of life for visitors and Londoners alike, suddenly became easy with the construction of a clean, efficient, comfortable airport express service from Paddington Station. (The price paid, seemingly, was the airportization and uglification of Brunel's Paddington Station, once one of the noblest old Victorian stations, now the predictable hideous conglomeration of glass, sushi bars, sock shops and cash-dispensing machines.)

If it was possible to construct such a good train service to the airport, why could not London have an Underground system to match that of Paris or Moscow? The answer must be found in the old question, unresolved since the Local Government Act of 1888, of how London is governed and of the relationship between London's local administrators and central government.

———

In an interview posthumously published, the historian Hugh Trevor-Roper (Lord Dacre) bewailed the "Americanization and moronization" of Britain, a phenomenon gleefully abetted by the newspaper magnate Rupert Murdoch. Anyone who has observed Britain over the last fifty years will know what he meant, and anyone who has lived in London for the last twenty years will know that the capital city is an organic expression of this moronization. Three examples must suffice.

On December 31, 1999, the eve of the new millennium, the Sovereign, the Prime Minister, and a great crowd of notables assembled for a mindless pop concert beneath the Dome that had been built in Greenwich. Enthusiasts for this ugly, and above all silly, building told us in advance that it would rival the Crystal Palace and the Great Exhibition of 1851, both in the profit it made and in the luster it shed upon the nation's reputation. At the time of writing, it still stands, but it stands empty, costing the taxpayer hundreds of millions of pounds. I was among the disconsolate 3 million who were conned into visiting the Greenwich site and finding that there was nothing in it but silliness. The Astronomical "Zone" told you far less about outer space than the excellent planetarium in the Marylebone Road; the Money Zone was conceived on a level so elementary as to insult the intelligence of the youngest child; the Faith

Zone, which had to be paid for by a pair of Hindu businessmen, who subsequently obtained British citizenship, was a pathetic travesty of Christian history. The most revealing feature of the whole place was its poor catering. One dreary pub, serving not especially nice food, was the only place where you could obtain alcohol; for the rest, it was pseudo- or actually American "fast food" joints. This was supposed to be a celebration of Britain, but it had not caught up with the revival of interest in British food, organically produced meats and vegetables, good English cheese, and real ales.

If the Dome made London a laughingstock, the conversion of the redundant Bankside Power Station into the Tate Modern was more risible, more pathetic. At least all the visitors to the Dome were able to see, once they had arrived there, that they had been conned and that the exhibits were absurd. The Bankside Power Station, which opened in 1963, was one of the last great works of functional architecture in London, built by Mott Hay and Anderson as engineers with the guiding architectural genius of Sir Giles Gilbert Scott, he of Liverpool Cathedral and the red telephone boxes. The brickwork is stunning, the spatial interiors worthy of some of the great Roman churches. It would have been an inspired idea to make the power station, when redundant, into an art gallery. Unfortunately, what it became was an advertisement for the fact that there was no art to put in it. Millions of visitors too scared to say that they did not know what art was flocked there and declared themselves excited, stimulated, and uplifted by the overpriced jokes perpetrated on the art world by clever "artists" and their dealers.

The third example of the moronization of London was the announcement in April 1996, by the dynamic and newly elected leader of the Labour Party, Tony Blair, that if his party were to win the next general election, he would introduce an American-style elected mayor for London. What followed, when Labour was duly elected the following year, outstripped the most satirical dreams of parodists. The Greater London Authority Act 1999 created the framework for an elected mayor and an Assembly of twenty-five members. Ken Livingstone, the nasal-voiced newt fancier who had made such a mess of being leader of the GLC, wanted to be the Labour candidate. The Prime Minister thought otherwise. Blair put in a stooge Labour candidate, the former leader of Camden Council, a bearded old dullard called Frank Dobson (Dobbo). He was not the People's Choice. In an election in which barely half the electorate chose to vote, Dobbo and his young puppetmaster in Downing Street were humiliated. The Tories fielded an amiable philanderer called Steve Norris. Livingstone stood as an independent candidate and won.

The London mayoralty has so far been the dismal failure which could have been predicted. Tony Blair liked speaking of democracy but he had no democratic instincts. The mayor was given an Assembly, and an ugly new building to replace Aston Webb's County Hall (which has been bought by the advertising mogul Charles Saatchi to house his notorious collection of dead sheep, unmade beds, and other artworks). But the mayor was given no power to raise tax, and therefore no real authority.

The central government refused to fund Livingstone's scheme to keep the London Underground in full public ownership and it insisted upon a scheme of public–private partnership, which the American transport supremo in charge of revitalizing the Tube, Bob Kiley, has declared unworkable. It is too early to say, at the time of writing, whether Ken Livingstone's congestion charges, designed to reduce traffic in the West End, will be a success. The difficulty of registering, to make oneself eligible to pay the charge of £5 per day, has dramatically reduced traffic in central London. In consequence, revenues from the scheme, to supply the much vaunted improvement in public transport, have been lacking. The scheme has been kindly described as a victim of its own success: this is what others would term a failure.

Livingstone's London Plan, published in the summer of 2002, is a masterpiece of ill-disguised euphemisms and clichés. "In the emerging information society London will need to become increasingly a learning city" (p. 30) is a piece of gobbledegook trying to hide from itself the fact that half the population of London will in future be illiterate. It points to the decline of manufacturing and says that the main "driver of jobs creation has been ... services primarily dominated by the leisure and people-orientated services sector." This means that very few Londoners any longer make or do anything specifically useful and that your best chance of a job, if you are unemployed, is work as a waiter, a domestic servant in a hotel, or a prostitute. The elected mayor feels it his duty to "tackle disadvantage—particularly among groups including women, disabled people and black and minority ethnic communities" (p. 15). Building a London that is "more accessible to disabled people" (p. 10) and "delivering the vision" will perhaps prove more of a challenge than "tackling" (a beloved word) the problem of unemployment. The mayor's plan notes that "29 per cent of working age adults in London are non-employed.... The rate is much higher for London's ethnic minorities, at 42 per cent" (p. 33). He makes no mention of the "black economy": no Londoner ever employs plasterers, decorators, carpenters, plumbers, or electricians, except in an emergency, in a manner that could be detected by the taxman. These individuals charge cash, as do most domestic cleaners and childminders or nannies, a high proportion of whom supplement their income by claiming unemployment or disability allowances. Not to do so would mean, quite simply, that they could not afford to live in London, where adequate rented property is hard to get and where purchasing even the smallest bedsit is beyond the financial reach of anyone trying to live on the pay of a teacher, a nurse, a firefighter, or a policeman.

What Ken Livingstone's Plan for London is saying, when you translate it into English and study its many tables of statistics, is that London is a city sustained by two economic factors: the City, upon whose financial and civic institutions Livingstone waged unceasing warfare in his GLC days; and tourism, which has changed the character of old London to the point of destroying it. If you add up the numbers of those in useful employment—employment remunerative enough to pay substantial tax, to finance the transport, health, educational, and welfare schemes on an even minimal level—you find that most of the inhabitants of Cool Britannia or Swinging London are drones, being kept by a diminishing group of overpaid businessmen, financiers, journalists, art dealers, and pop musicians. This is the vision which the ever popular Red Ken was able to deliver to an indifferent populace in hundreds of pages of scarcely readable prose.

While giving due attention to the wonders of the Blue Ribbon Network (the London waterways), with an estimated 3 million people and 750,000 tons of household waste being floated at various junctures of the year down the River Thames, Ken hesitates to spell out the implications of global warming, and what provision is to be made against flooding should the ocean and the river rise above the modest levels predicted years ago at the time of the building of the Thames barrier. The Environment Agency believes that it would cost London taxpayers more than £4 billion over the next few years to stop the Thames flooding. In the autumn and winter since their report of 2002, Thameside areas such as parts of Surrey and Berkshire (for example, Maidenhead) have suffered flooding more severe than ever in their history. Ken has given the go-ahead for 100,000 new properties to be built in the Thames Gateway region, east of London. Sadly, the Association of British Insurers, in the person of their spokesman Mr. Malcolm Tarling, has said, "We would have to start thinking about moving our capital city elsewhere." This is apocalyptic talk, as is the statement of the aptly named Mike Tempest of Thames Water, who says that it would cost "billions of pounds" to give the capital adequate drainage and sewage.

London certainly faces grave problems, if its population continues to expand and its infrastructure remains underfunded. No doubt there are Jeremiahs who believe that it is ill equipped for the future; and the flood warnings must prompt in some minds the belief that London will itself be swept beneath the waves, to be at one with Nineveh and Tyre.

And yet there is something about modern London which makes one believe that, in spite of all the mistakes made by its administrators, it will meet the challenges of the future. The very fact that so many people want to come to London is a guarantee of its ebullient and irrepressible life.

They do not come simply as spongers and criminals, as pessimists try to make us believe. People are drawn to London, from other parts of the United Kingdom, as from abroad, excited by a collective energy that is palpable, and by the fact that so much of what is going on in modern London is good. Investors show no signs of deserting the City. In spite of the moronization of the capital by publicists and politicians, there has never been a time when the museums and galleries were putting on exhibitions of a higher standard, or when the restaurants were better. The standard of the London theaters, and supremely of the Royal Opera House and Royal Ballet, the quality of concerts in innumerable venues, both for classical and for every other kind of music, can easily rival, and often outstrip Paris, New York, or Milan. Shopping in London could easily be, and for some people is, a full-time occupation. Nightlife caters for every taste, however innocent or dissipated. You feel alive in London, as nowhere else in Britain, surrounded by so much excellence.

Equally, for all the ugliness of buildings and road developments that have been hurled together without thought, London remains a city of great elegance. As you walk from one quarter of it to the next, you pass every few hundred yards what would be, in any other part of the United Kingdom, a townscape to make a fuss about. The medieval buildings of Westminster and of Smithfield are breathtaking, as is the Tower. Despite the frenzy of aerial bombardment and the greed of property developers, there are still beautiful seventeenth- and eighteenth-century churches; there is still an abundance of superb squares and terraces of the eighteenth and nineteenth centuries. Our generation has perhaps not contributed much to the architecture of London of which future generations will be proud, but who knows, the works of Lord Rogers may one day be as revered as Street's Law Courts, Barry's Palace of Westminster or Charles Holden's Senate House.

An architectural tour of London is, in any event, so much more than merely an aesthetic experience. It is a personal encounter with Londoners of the past. Every district of London, whether or not it is on the tourist map, is haunted by memories. The past and the present are always blended here. In the crowds of present-day London, we can see the faces of those who "flowed over London Bridge" in previous generations. In the ever fluctuating population, we sense that the life of the city is a collective experience, partly secret and partly shared. It is shared not just by the living, but also with the dead. The dynamism, its unquenchable life, stretching towards an unseen future, derives largely from the past, and from the multiplicity of human experiences that the streets and rivers of London have witnessed since the Romans first built their makeshift bridge somewhere near modern Westminster.

A CHRONOLOGY
OF LONDON HISTORY

A.D. **43** Aulus Plautius, victorious over native forces, built a bridge over the Thames. Encamped near modern Westminster, where he was joined by the Emperor Claudius. Londinium established by the Romans.

60 Rebellion of the Iceni under Queen Boadicea. Huge casualties. The Romans triumphant.

61–122 Londinium built as a great city.

c. 400 Arrival of Germanic tribes in Britain. Gradual withdrawal of Romans and decline of London.

597 St. Augustine's mission to England.

604 Establishment of Christian bishopric and of the first St. Paul's Cathedral in London.

1066 Norman Conquest. William I crowned at Westminster. The White Tower built as a Norman keep.

1097–99 Westminster Hall built, center of the royal court.

1189 First mayor of London, Henry FitzAilwin.

1221 Completion of old St. Paul's Cathedral tower and steeple.

1245–69 Rebuilding of Westminster Abbey by Henry III.

1377–99 Reign of Richard II. London's heyday, with Chaucer, Gower, and Langland all writing and the Wilton Diptych being painted. Enormous wealth from the wool trade.

1381 Peasant's Revolt. John Ball leads rebels in a huge crowd over London Bridge. Rebellion suppressed.

1476 Caxton establishes his printing press in London.

1509 St. Paul's School founded by John Colet.

1535 Three Carthusian friars hanged at Tyburn. London Charterhouse closed in 1537 and later passed to Sir Edward North. It would eventually (1614) house Charterhouse School.

1554–88 More than 200 Protestant martyrs burned at Smithfield.

1561 Merchant Taylor's School founded in Suffolk Lane.

1570 Royal Exchange opened by Queen Elizabeth I.

1598–99 The Globe Theatre built on Bankside by Cuthbert and Richard Burbage, showing many of Shakespeare's plays. Closed in 1642 by Puritans.

1615 Inigo Jones surveyor-general of the works. Designed Queen's House, Greenwich (finished 1635), a new Banqueting House (finished 1622), a new Palace of Whitehall (never built), restorations and changes to St. Paul's Cathedral, and the rebuilding of Covent Garden (completed 1639).

January 30, 1649 Execution of King Charles I outside the Banqueting House, Whitehall.

November 1660 The Royal Society formally constituted (charter 1662).

September 2, 1666 The Great Fire began in Pudding Lane, just east of London Bridge. Losses include 13,200 houses and many public buildings, including churches, Christ's Hospital, Newgate Prison, and Baynard's Castle. The Guildhall was gutted. St. Paul's a near ruin. A vast rebuilding program is undertaken in the following years.

1694 The Bank of England Act establishes a national bank and a national debt.

1710 St. Paul's Cathedral completed.

1720 Westminster Hospital established. Followed by four other general hospitals: Guy's (1725), St. George's (1733), the London Hospital (1740), and the Middlesex (1745).

September 1720 The South Sea Bubble bursts, in one of the first major crises of capitalism.

1714–29 Hawkmoor's magnificent Christ Church Spitalfields erected in an area fast filling with Huguenot weavers. The center of the silk-weaving industry.

June 2, 1780 The riots led by Lord George Gordon in protest against the repeal of anti-Catholic legislation. Several private embassy chapels destroyed and Newgate, Clerkenwell, Fleet, King's Bench, and Borough Clink prisons burned down.

July 1829 The Metropolitan Police Bill, the brainchild of Sir Robert Peel, introduces a police force for the capital.

April 10, 1848 Chartist rally on Kennington Common. The Royal family sent to the Isle of Wight for their own safety. The Bank of England and Somerset House sandbagged and some 85,000 special constables enlisted against the agitations for one man, one vote. Although 100,000 Chartists were expected, fewer than 20,000 attended.

1851 The Great Exhibition in Hyde Park.

1863 Metropolitan Railway, the first steam-operated Underground, opened. The first electric railway through steel tunnels ran in 1870.

1868 Completion of Joseph Bazalgette's sewer plan at a cost of £4.6 million; 82 miles of pipes deposit 52 million gallons of rainwater and untreated sewage into the Thames each day.

1880s and 1890s Growth of large West End department stores imitating William Whiteley of Westbourne Grove: Dickins & Jones, Marshall & Snelgrove, Swan & Edgar, Debenham & Freebody.

1889 Sir William Harcourt, Home Secretary in Lord Salisbury's Conservative government, creates the London County Council (LCC). London is described by Sidney Webb as "a genuine self-governing community."

August 3, 1914 Last day of peace before the Great War. Large crowds assemble to cheer the King outside Buckingham Palace.

The Prime Minsister, Asquith, remarks, "War is always popular with the London mob."

May 31, 1915 First air raids by Zeppelin airships on the docks and the City.

1931 Royal Commission on Transport declares that trams are "in a state of obsolescence." They are gradually phased out.

October 1932 The British Union of Fascists hold its first rally in Trafalgar Square. They never win a parliamentary seat.

1939–45 Second World War. Fears on the outbreak of war that hundreds of thousands of Londoners would be killed were exaggerated: 29,890 were killed by air raids and 50,000 badly injured. Inspired by Churchill and the King and Queen, Londoners pluckily survive the years of bombs and blackouts.

1951 The Festival of Britain.

1956 The Clean Air Act. It did not cure the famous London fogs ("pea-soupers") instantly. In December 1957, fog caused a major rail disaster at Lewisham in which 87 lost their lives.

December 1962 The last real pea-souper.

1958 Notting Hill race riots.

1963 The London Government Bill. GLC bigger, but weaker, than the old LCC. The Inner London Education Authority (ILEA) area defined.

1986 Abolition of GLC by Margaret Thatcher.

October 27, 1986 "Big Bang" abolishes fixed commissions and opens the renamed International Stock Market to foreign companies, allowing the formation of very large merchant banking and brokerage houses and introducing electronic dealing.

1999 Greater London Authority Act creates a framework for an elected mayor and twenty-five elected members of a council. The first elected mayor is Ken Livingstone, an independent candidate who defeats both Tories and Labour.

Notes

2 New Troy or Roman London?

1. William Maitland, *The History of London* (1775), p. 137.
2. *Dictionary of National Biography.*
3. Geoffrey of Monmouth, *The History of the Kings of Britain*, trans. Lewis Thorpe (Penguin, 1966), p. 65.

4 Chaucer's London

1. City Hustings Roll 110, 5, Richard II membrane 2.

5 Tudor and Stuart London

1. Katherine Duncan-Jones, *Ungentle Shakespeare* (Arden, 2001), p. 58.
2. Roy Porter, *London: A Social History*, p. 16.
3. Charles Lethbridge Kingsford, introduction to John Stow, *A Survey of London* (Oxford University Press, 1908).

7 GEORGIAN

1. John Carswell, *The South Sea Bubble* (Cresset Press, 1960), pp. 198–99.
2. Antonia Fraser, *Cromwell* (Weidenfeld & Nicolson, 1973), p. 561.

8 THE INDUSTRIAL REVOLUTION AND THE METROPOLIS OF NASH

1. Quoted by Martin Daunton in C. Fox (ed.), *London: World City 1800–1840* (Yale University Press with Museum of London, 1992), p. 21.
2. See Andrew Saint, "The Building Art of the First Industrial Metropolis" and Martin Daunton, "London and the World" in C. Fox, op. cit.
3. Susan Lasdun, *The English Park* (André Deutsch, 1991), p. 177.

10 1900–1939

1. Ruth Guilding, "The Model Traffic Recreation Area at Lordship Lane," p. 18.
2. Anthony Grenville, *Continental Britons: Jewish Refugees from Nazi Europe* (The Jewish Museum, London, 2002), p. 30.
3. Harold Nicolson, *Diaries, 1930–39* (Collins, 1971), p. 413.
4. Quoted in Philip Ziegler, *London at War 1939–1945* (Sinclair-Stevenson, 1995), p. 11.

11 WARTIME 1939–1945

1. William Shakespeare, *King John,* Act V, scene vii, ll. 112–13.
2. Simone Pétrement, *Simone Weil* (Mowbrays, 1976), p. 511.
3. Alexandra Richie, *Faust's Metropolis* (HarperCollins, 1998), p. 496.
4. Elizabeth Bowen, *The Heat of the Day* (Jonathan Cape, 1949), p. 83.

5. Stephen Inwood, *A History of London* (Macmillan, 1998), p. 781. Francis Sheppard, *London: A History* (Oxford, 1998), p. 334.
6. Conversation with the author.
7. *Don Juan,* Canto IX.iv.

12 POSTWAR

1. See Robert Gray, *A History of London,* p. 318.
2. William J. R. Curtis, *Denys Lasdun: Architecture, City, Landscape* (Phaidon, 1994).
3. Mike Pentelow and Marsha Rowe, *Characters of Fitzrovia* (Chatto, 2001), p. 236.

13 THE END OF THE BOWLER HAT

1. Peter Walker, *Staying Power* (1991), p. 56. Quoted in David Kynaston, *The City of London,* vol. 4: *A Club No More 1945–2000.*
2. Quoted in Kynaston (see note 1, above), p. 696.
3. *Gulliver's Travels,* Part III, chapter 5.
4. Jerry White, *London in the Twentieth Century,* p. 342.

14 LONDON COSMOPOLIS

1 BBC News website, "Immigration: Fact or Hype," August 2002.
2. The Draft London Plan, p. 15.

15 SILLY LONDON

1. Edward Gibbon, *The Decline and Fall of the Roman Empire,* chapter 52.

Select Bibliography

The bibliography of London histories is enormous. What follows is only a selection of works I consulted.

Ackroyd, Peter. *London: The Biography.* Chatto, 2000

Ashton, John. *The Fleet: Its River, Prison and Marriages.* T. Fisher Unwin, 1888

Baker, Timothy. *Medieval London.* Cassell, 1970

Barnett, David. *London, Hub of the Industrial Revolution.* Tauris Academic Studies, 1998

Barton, N. J. *The Lost Rivers of London.* Phoenix House, London, Leicester University Press, 1962

Betjeman, John. *London's Historic Railway Stations.* John Murray, 1978

———. *Metroland.* Warren, 1977

———. *Summoned by Bells.* John Murray, 1966

———. *Victorian and Edwardian London from Old Photographs.* Portman, 1987

Boswell, James. *Life of Johnson.* Everyman, 1992

Bowen, Elizabeth. *The Heat of the Day.* Jonathan Cape, 1949

Brimblecombe, Peter. *The Big Smoke: A History of Air Pollution in London Since Medieval Times.* Routledge, 1988

Byrne, Andrew. *London's Georgian Houses.* Georgian Press, 1986

Byrne, Richard. *Prisons and Punishments of London.* Harrap, 1981

Chapman, Stanley. *The Rise of Merchant Banking.* Allen and Unwin, 1984

Clark, John. *Saxon and Norman London.* HMSO, 1989

Clayton, Anthony. *Subterranean City.* London Historical Publications, 2000

Clout, Hugh, ed. *The Times London Atlas.* The Times (London), 1991

Cole, Harry. *Policeman's Lot.* Fontana, 1981

Cruickshank, Dan, and Neil Burton. *Life in the Georgian City.* Viking, 1990

Cruickshank, Dan, and Peter Wyld. *Georgian Town Houses and Their Details,* Butterworth, 1990

———. *London: The Art of Georgian Building.* Architectural Press, 1975

Dakers, Caroline. *The Holland Park Circle.* Yale University Press, 1999

De Mare, Eric. *Wren's London.* Michael Joseph, 1975

Denton, Pennie, ed. *Betjeman's London.* John Murray, 1988

Duffy, Ian. *Bankruptcy and Insolvency in London During the Industrial Revolution.* Garland, 1985

Elgar, Donald. *The Royal Parks.* W. H. Allen, 1986

Eliot, T. S. *Collected Poems 1909–1962.* Faber, 1963

Eylse, Allen, and Keith Skone. *London's West End Cinemas.* Sutton, Premier Bioscope, 1984

Fido, Martin. *Murder Guide to London.* Grafton, 1990

Fox, Celina, ed. *London: World City 1800–1840.* Yale University Press in association with the Museum of London, 1992

George, M. Dorothy. *London Life in the Eighteenth Century.* Penguin, 1976

———. *Nursing at Guy's 1726–1996.* Granta Editions, 1997

Girouard, Mark. *Victorian Pubs.* Studio Vista, 1975

Goodway, David. *London Chartism 1838–1848.* Cambridge University Press, 1982

Gray, Robert. *A History of London.* Hutchinson, 1978

Guilding, Ruth. "The Model Traffic Recreation Area at Lordship Lane." *The London Gardener or the Gardener's Intelligence,* vol. 2, no. 2 (1996–97), p. 18.

Halliday, Stephen. *The Great Stink of London.* Sutton, Stroud, 2001

Hammond, Peter. *Her Majesty's Royal Palace and Fortress of the Tower of London.* Department of the Environment, 1987

Harrison, Michael. *London Beneath the Pavement.* Peter Davies, 1961

Hibbert, Christopher. *London: The Biography of a City.* Penguin, 1980

Hone, J. Ann. *For the Cause of Truth: Radicalism in London.* Oxford, 1982

Howe, Ellie. *A Short Guide to the Fleet River.* T. C. Thompson & Son, 1955

Howson, H. F. *London's Underground.* Ian Allan, 1981

Huelin, Gordon. *Vanished Churches of the City of London.* Guidhall Library, 1996

Inwood, Stephen. *A History of London.* Macmillan, 1998

Jones, Gareth Stedman. *Outcast London.* Penguin, 1976

Knott, Simon. *The Electoral Crucible: The Politics of London 1900–1914.* Greene & Co., 1977

Knott, Simon. *The Zoological Society of London, 1826–1876.* Zoological Society of London, 1976

Kynaston, David. *The City of London.* Vol. 1: *A World of Its Own, 1815–1890;* vol. 2: *Golden Years, 1890–1914;* vol. 3: *Illusions of Gold, 1914–1945;* vol. 4: *A Club No More, 1945–2000.* Chatto: 1994–2001

Lasdun, Susan. *The English Park: Royal, Private and Public.* André Deutsch, 1991

Lindsay, Paul. *The Synagogues of London.* Vallentine Mitchell, 1993

Linebaugh, Peter. *The London Hanged.* Allen Lane, 1991

Longstaffe-Gowan, Todd. *The London Town Garden, 1740–1840.* Yale University Press, 2001

Marsden, Peter. *Londonium.* Ginn, 1971

Matthews, John and Chesca Potter, eds. *The Antiquarian Guide to Legendary London*. The Aquarian Press, 1990

McKellar, Elizabeth. *The Birth of Modern London*. Manchester University Press, 1999

McKisack, May. *The Fourteenth Century*. Oxford at the Clarendon Press, 1959

Mears, Kenneth. *The Tower of London: Nine Hundred Years of English History*. Phaidon, 1988

Merrifield, Ralph. *Roman London*. Cassell, 1969

Milne, Gustav. *The Port of Roman London*. Batsford, 1985

Okokon, Susan. *Black Londoners, 1880–1990*. Sutton, Stroud, 1998

Olsen, Donald. *The Growth of Victorian London*. Penguin, 1979

Orwell, George. *The Collected Essays, Journalism and Letters*. Vol. 1, Penguin, 1983

Pennick, Nigel. *Early Tube Railways of London*. Electric Traction Publications, undated

Pevsner, Nikolaus. *London*. 2 vols. Revised by Bridget Cherry, Weidenfeld & Nicholson

Porter, Roy. *London: A Social History*. Hamish Hamilton, 1994

Potter, Chesen, website, *The River of Walls*

Riley, Henry Thomas, ed. *Munimenta Gildhallae Londoniensis*. Vols. I and III. Longman, 1859

Rivett, Geoffrey. *The Development of the London Hospital System, 1823–1982*. King Edward's Hospital Fund for London, 1986

Rowse, A. L. *The Tower of London*. Michael Joseph, 1977

Schofield, John. *The Building of London, from the Conquest to the Great Fire*. Bristol Museum Publications, 1984

Shaw, E. R. *The London Money Market*. Heinemann, 1978

Sheppard, Francis. *London: A History*. Oxford University Press, 1998

Shute, Narina. *London Villages*. Hale, 1977

Stamp, Gavin. *The Changing Metropolis*. Viking, 1984

Stevenson, John, ed. *London in the Age of Reform*. Blackwell, 1977

Summerson, John. *Georgian London.* 1948; revised edition, Penguin, 1978

Taylor, Gladys. *Old London Gardens.* Hornchurch, 1977

Thomson, David. *In Camden Town.* Hutchinson, 1983

Tyndale, Timothy. *The Lawyers, the Inns of Court: The Home of the Common Law.* Wildy & Sons, 1976

White, Jerry. *London in the Twentieth Century.* Viking, 2001

———. *The Worst Street in North London: Campbell Bunk Islington Between the Wars.* Routledge, 1986

Willson, E. J., *West London Nursery Gardens.* Fulham and Hammersmith Historical Society, 1982

Yelling, J. A. *Slums and Slum Clearance in Victorian London.* Allen and Unwin 1986

INDEX